Memoir of a Mascot

Life as the Penn Quaker

Brian Becker

**Independently published
by Brian Becker**
Copyright © 2023 by Brian Becker
ISBN 979-8-218-23249-8

Cover photo: Courtesy of the University of Pennsylvania 1984 Yearbook, Poor Richard's Record as cropped and quasi-colorized by the author.

ACKNOWLEDGMENTS

Thanks to Eric Jacobs, General Manager of the DP and Mark Lloyd, Director of the Penn Archives for their assistance in obtaining permissions and guidance on using previously published articles and photos. In exchange, I promised to donate a portion of the proceeds to the DP if this book makes it to The New York Times bestseller list (and even though I didn't promise to do so, in the event of the same occurrence, I will also donate to the University for use of the yearbook photos).

Thanks to Paul Jolovitz for speaking with me late at night to revisit the interview during the Fleet Classic and for trying to obtain the audio of that interview. I subsequently found a cassette tape of the interview mixed in with a bunch of other cassette recordings I had stored away and completely forgotten about.

Thanks to Tim Mclaughlin and Mike Mahoney of the Penn Athletic Department for their help in obtaining the picture of the streamers flying in the Palestra and the rights to use it in this book.

Thanks to photographer Adam Smith for permission to use the photo of the University of Pennsylvania Quadrangle.

Thanks to my parents for guiding me through childhood and inspiring me to do my best in school and in life.

Thanks to my housemates, classmates, and fans at Penn for their support and encouragement during my time as the Quaker.

Thanks to everyone who gave me permission to use their images in the photos included in this book.

Thanks to my sons, Casey and Cary, for their helpful editorial comments and their proofreading the manuscript.

And finally, last but most certainly not least, special thanks to my wife, the love of my life, for her patience in allowing me the time to write this book, for her encouragement and insightful comments on my drafts and for always standing beside me as my best friend and the best partner anyone could ever dream of having.

Table of Contents

Introduction

I had the honor of being the mascot of the University of Pennsylvania, the Quaker, during my senior year at Penn. Over the nearly forty years since my graduation in May 1984, I have been asked many times about my mascot experience. How did you become the mascot? What was it like? What did you do? In response, I recounted several stories – all true – much to the delight of my listeners.

This book is my attempt to collect those stories – and more – all in one place. I have done my best to be as accurate as possible but being nearly forty years removed from the experience, you'll have to forgive me if a detail or two didn't happen exactly as I remember it. Also, apart from those individuals well-known publicly, at least at Penn, I have decided to use only first names for the people appearing in this book (and even changed a few names altogether) to protect the innocent among them and to give the others plausible deniability.

Despite any help I may have received from others in editing, any mistakes remaining are my own. This book was fun for me to write. I hope you enjoy reading it.

Chapter 1 – And So It Begins

Hunched over a thick textbook in my first floor, poster-covered dorm room in the Quad[1] of the University of Pennsylvania, I shot upright when a sudden knock on my open door shattered the silence. Brooke, the petite, blonde resident advisor – and the dream girl of most guys on my floor – stood in the doorway wearing short red shorts, a tight white t-shirt, and a smile from ear to ear. She was recruiting.

"Hi, Brian! Watcha doin'?" she chirped with a slight Philly accent. She continued beaming while waiting for a response.

I just stared at her. "Ya know," she said with a pause, "We really need more male cheerleaders to join the squad."

"Well, you're talking to the wrong guy, Brooke. I'm a band lunatic! I don't want to be a cheerleader," I retorted. Most people knew the band and the cheerleaders didn't particularly get along. As Brooke's beaming smile began to fade, I added, without really thinking, "I'd only leave the band if I could be the *official* school fool!"

---

[1] The Quad is a residence hall composed of thirty-nine conjoined brick gargoyle-bearing buildings housing about fifteen hundred students.

Brooke's fading smile reappeared even broader than before, and she excitedly proclaimed. "Well then, you should try out for the Quaker!" And so it began in the spring of 1982. Brooke, the senior cheerleader, took Brian, a sophomore alto sax player in the band, to cheerleading tryouts later that evening.

Sun setting on our backs, Brooke and I walked briskly through the cool spring air from the Quad down Spruce Street to 33rd. We turned left, crossed the street, and passed the mammoth 74,000-seat football stadium, Franklin Field,[2] looming to our right.

As we walked, I asked Brooke, "So what is it exactly I'm going to have to do?"

"A bunch of different stuff. You'll see," she replied. "It's really up to the captains."

Just past the stadium, we turned right, and made our way to the squat reddish-brown brick building accented by off-white sandstone stripes. Tryouts were being held in the Palestra, home court of the Penn Quaker basketball teams and the most storied gymnasium in the history of collegiate athletics.[3]

---

[2] Penn's Franklin Field is the university's venerable football/track stadium. Built in 1895, it is the oldest college football stadium in the country and home, not only to Penn's football team but also to the Penn Relays – the oldest and largest track and field competition in the United States. Franklin Field also served as the home field for the NFL's Philadelphia Eagles from 1958-1970.

[3] Known as "the Cathedral of College Basketball," much has been said and written about the Palestra. "I don't think there's a place on earth that is comparable to it," said Les Keiter, the voice of the Big 5 during the 1960's. "I've broadcasted games all over the world and no matter where I was, I

Arched doorways led into the facility.   As we walked in, our eyes adjusted to the dimly lit, wide hallway. On each side were display cases showing plaques and pictures of memorable events, sports stars, coaches, and broadcasters who played or worked for one of the local teams. One display case even held a football from the 1917 New Year's Day Rose Bowl game that Penn lost to Oregon 14-0.

My pulse quickened as we walked up the ramp and I took my first steps onto the brightly lit floor of the arena. Wooden bleachers that could seat 9000 screaming souls surrounded us on all four sides. Above us, heavy steel archways stretching from side to side held the roof high and sported red and blue banners celebrating past Penn athletic achievements. The large scoreboards on either end were dark.

At center court were the male and female co-captains and co-captains-elect of the cheerleading squad. They, together with an athletic department administrator, Ms. Dunflap, were the judges who would choose the members of the squad for the next academic year.   Milling about them were seventy or so young

---

would always say, 'You don't know what it's like until you walk into the Palestra.' You talk about the Field of Dreams in baseball, this was my Field of Dreams. The mystique and the history of the place are unparalleled. When you first come through the doors there's a certain feeling that you get that just transcends the moment. Then you walk out on the floor and look up at nine thousand people, the scoreboard, the streamers, the fervor and fever in the stands, the intensity of the players and the coaches. There's nothing like it in the world of sports. It almost defies description."
(Excerpt taken from "*Palestra Pandemonium, A History of the Big Five*", by author Bob Lyons)

men and women in shorts and t-shirts waiting for the tryouts to begin.

"All right everyone. Have a seat right here," said Alejandro, the outgoing male co-captain pointing to the floor in front of him. After everyone settled down, he continued, "Here's how this is going to work. Over the next three weeks, we're going to teach you the cheers, the carefully choreographed moves that go with the cheers, how to safely build and take down human pyramids and how to perform other stunts."

"We'll be holding practices three nights a week, with final tryouts taking place on the last two nights of the third week," he continued. "By a show of hands, how many of you are interested in trying out for Quaker?" I raised my hand and noticed two other men raised their hands, too.

"Well, gentlemen," Alejandro said while moving his eyes from face to face among us, "each of you will need to learn the cheers, how to help build the pyramid, how to spot the women cheerleaders when they are being held up in the air by their partners and when they are at the top of the pyramid. You also will be asked, from time to time, to make some signs that you would hold up at different games during the season. You, too, will be asked to show us how well you can perform the choreographed cheers at the end of tryouts. Good luck everybody. Let's get started."

From that point, we spent three nights a week for the next three weeks singing and learning the cheerleading moves to the Penn songs: Fight On, Pennsylvania; Cheer Pennsylvania, and The Red and Blue. I had the built-in advantage of already knowing the words and melodies of all the songs from my time in the

Penn Band. That just left learning the cheerleading moves to those songs.

To me, it just seemed like a lot of flailing. For example, the moves used during the Red and Blue included a combination of crisscrossing arms, raising them at right angles, dropping them along your sides, and bringing your fists together across your chest with arms level to the ground, while occasionally taking small steps forward with your right foot and then rocking back while extending your arms in front of you until both your feet are once again side by side. You finished by extending your right arm across your body and then fully extending it out to your right side (this would be how you would lead the crowd at a game to keep them moving their arms in unison in the right direction).[4] Not hard to master, just a little tedious to be practicing again and again, night after night.

Fred and Phil, the other two Quaker wannabes, and I also took turns helping female cheerleader candidates make their way up the human pyramids and helping to catch the women at the top who would fall backward into our waiting arms at the tail end of the stunt. And so it went. There was no opportunity for any

---

[4] They say a picture's worth a thousand words, so I figure a video has got to be worth at least a few more! I found this one where you can see us performing the moves to the Red and Blue at the end of a basketball game. Go to http://letsgoquakers.com/basketball1980s.htm and then scroll down until you find the entry below. Once there, simply click on the video camera in the second to last column. The moves described begin at about the 1:40 mark of the video. Enjoy!

| 03/03/1984 | YALE | W 63-60 | FINAL 0:12 ONLY | UTV-13 | DAN LIEBERMAN ANDY SPARK | DVD | | 0:04:00 |

of the Quaker finalists to distinguish himself from any of the others. The only difference was I was the only sophomore.

And so, three weeks later when the call came and I was informed that Fred had been selected as the Quaker, the main reason given was that traditionally the job had been given to an incoming senior. When Brooke came to my room to convey her condolences, I expressed my disappointment by asking, "Why couldn't they have just told me at the beginning that they would be giving it to a senior? Why waste my time?"

Brooke just shrugged, thanked me for trying out, gave me a hug and said, "You can always try again next year!"

"Right," I said sarcastically. "I don't think so. At least now, I won't be leaving the band." Or so I thought. Silly me.

Chapter 2 – Tryouts Take Two, Part One

Unfortunately for Fred, when he took to the field as the Quaker, he appeared to have a bad case of stage fright and there was no hiding from it. The Quaker back then, unlike many other mascots, was not an anonymous person hidden by an enlarged costume head. The Quaker's costume consisted of a black three-cornered hat with a white stripe around its folded brim, a white peasant shirt covered by a purplish waistcoat, a ruffled white jabot, and a mid-thigh length dark red coat with lacy cuffs protruding from the sleeves, blue breeches that snapped closed just below the knees, high white stockings, and sneakers. As a result, the face of the person playing the Quaker remained in plain sight for all to see.

All through the most exciting football season in three decades, culminating in David Shulman's kick with no time left on the clock to beat Harvard and give Penn a share of its first Ivy League championship since 1959[5], poor Fred couldn't overcome his shyness. During football games, he mostly stood along the sidelines as fans urged him to do something, anything, but to no avail. He was booed. He was jeered. It was sad. While a very nice guy, clearly Fred was not cut out for the job. I felt badly for him.

---

[5] Otherwise known as the Miracle on 33rd Street.

Things did not improve for Fred during basketball season either. My friends made comments to me such as, "You should try out again. We've got to have a better Quaker next year."

Apparently, a lot of other people felt the same way. As a result, when I arrived for tryouts in the spring of 1983 still feeling the sting from the prior year, there were a DOZEN other candidates – including one woman! To date, all the Quakers had been men.

"Damn," I thought to myself. "Instead of having to beat out just a couple of other guys, there's a whole bunch of people. This is going to be a colossal challenge."

Once again, tryouts were being held in the Palestra. Much of the tryout routine was the same as the year before. This time, however, about three days into tryouts, Steve and Kara, the co-captains-elect, revealed an additional aspect for the Quaker candidates. "One week from tonight," announced Kara, "each of you will take to center court and perform before the entire group of cheerleading candidates as though it were halftime of a basketball game." This was the chance to distinguish ourselves and show our creativity, humor, and showmanship.

Over the next week, I could think of little else. I spent hours in my third floor rowhouse bedroom trying to decide what I should do. I thought that whatever it was should be very visual as it needed to be something that could be performed before thousands. After spending many hours brainstorming and daydreaming while alternatively pacing back and forth between my dresser and a makeshift milk crate bookcase, sitting at my well-used and scratched metal elementary school desks[6]

---

[6] I had acquired the desks in the summer before I moved off campus for ten dollars at an elementary school sale.

tapping a pencil, and lying on my bed while staring at the ceiling, the idea struck me like a lightning bolt.

Over the next several days, I gathered the materials I would need as props and spent countless hours envisioning and refining each step of my performance. At night, I would dream about going out on the floor in front of seventy cheerleader wannabes and running through the routine I developed. But I would need an assistant.

On the night that the Quaker candidates were scheduled to perform, I arrived with my props and sought out one of the pretty women aspiring to be a cheerleader. "Laura, I have a favor to ask," I said in an undertone. "I've devised a skit but need an assistant. If you're willing to help me, I could explain what you need to do in about 30 seconds." Fortunately, she agreed, and I was ready.

Tryout practice began as usual with everyone going through the moves to the Penn songs, performing different cheerleading lifts, and coordinating on stunts. About an hour into the practice, co-captain Steve interrupted the proceedings. "O.k. everybody, take a seat on the side of the court," he directed. "It's time to let the Quaker candidates entertain us."

As everyone took a seat in the first couple of rows of the stands on one side of the court, Steve continued, "Now we'll call each Quaker finalist out, one at a time, and you'll each have your chance to perform. First up, Ralph."

Ralph took to the court and began juggling handkerchiefs. When he finished another candidate threw around a Nerf ball. Another tried telling jokes – which, of course, would never work at a real basketball game as he wouldn't be heard above the crowd noise. And so it went, act after act, until…

"Brian. Your turn," Steve announced.

With a suitcase in my left hand and a basketball tucked under my right arm, I walked quickly out to center court, turned to face the crowd, and knelt to put down the basketball and lay the suitcase on its side. I opened the top of suitcase enabling me to access what was inside it without any of the audience being able to see its contents. I removed a small stack of standard poster boards, on which I had used magic markers to create signs and laid them face down on the court a few feet from the suitcase.

Picking up the basketball, I announced, "I need an assistant." And then, pointing to Laura, I asked, "Would you please join me?" Having pre-arranged her participation, she jumped up and strode right out on the court over to the pile of poster board signs.

Laura raised the first sign that read, "Welcome to the Quaker's Traveling Basketball Clinic." People in the audience smiled. As Laura dropped the first sign and squatted down to pick up the second, adrenaline was coursing through my veins.

Laura stood up and raised the next sign that read: "The Quaker will first demonstrate how to make a simple layup." I dribbled the basketball from center court down to one of the baskets and made a simple layup, after which I returned to center court and squatted behind the open suitcase tinkering with something inside it as Laura was raising the next sign that read, "The Quaker will now demonstrate how to make a reverse layup." I ran to the basket, threw the ball off the backboard, caught it, and dribbled backwards toward center court. Cheesy, but it got a smattering of laughs from the crowd. Again, I returned to the suitcase and continued my tinkering.

The next sign read, "Next the Quaker will demonstrate the fine art of making a pass." With that, I walked over to Laura, cupped my hand to the side of my face and whispered into her ear. She slapped me in the face, and I staggered backward as Laura shook her head vigorously from side to side. Several people in the crowd chuckled as I made my way back to the suitcase and continued fiddling with its contents.

Laura raised the next sign that read, "Now, there is one thing you NEVER want to do when the game is on the line… and that's throw up a brick." As the audience was reading the sign, I grabbed an actual red brick out of the suitcase and quickly marched toward the basket stopping at the top of the key. I began swinging the brick in circles above my head readying to throw it at the basket. Just as I took another step toward the basket and was about to release the brick, Laura grabbed the brick with one hand and vigorously shook the forefinger of her other hand at me. I feigned dejection and walked, head down, back to the suitcase.

The next sign read, "One thing you ALWAYS want to do when the game is on the line is make all of your foul shots." Again, I marched quickly toward the basket, this time with a rubber chicken in hand. Stopping at the free throw line, I dribbled the springy fowl a couple of times and then launched it toward the basket. Much to my amazement, I made the shot! Not only that, but the chicken got stuck in the net adding to the hilarity of the moment and sparking guffaws from the audience. While making my way back to the suitcase, I couldn't help but notice co-captain Steve wiping his eyes and repeatedly slapping his knee while trying to breathe.

As Laura raised the final sign, which read, "No matter what else, here's a play that always gets the crowd going," I pulled my alto saxophone (which I had been assembling bit by bit with my mysterious tinkering throughout the routine) from the suitcase and began playing "Go, Team, Go." The seventy cheerleader wannabes in the audience, clapped along in rhythm. After playing in ascending notes, "bump, bump, bump, BAH-dup, bump, bump, bump, BAH-dup, bump, bump, bump, BAH-dup BUMP, BUMP BUMP!" everyone enthusiastically shouted, "GO, PENN, GO!" It was the perfect ending to the performance.

Now a week and a half into tryouts, I realized the first half of the ordeal was complete. Reflecting on the evening while striding quickly across the campus to my row house, suitcase in one hand and basketball in the other, I thought things had gone very well. Later that night, after I showered and the adrenaline had left my system, I flopped into bed exhausted and slept a good, deep sleep.

Chapter 3 – Tryouts Take Two, Part Two

At the next practice, everyone was still buzzing over the Quaker candidates' performances. At the mid-practice break, we were sitting on the floor along one side of the court chatting when I noticed Kara walking toward us from the far corner where the co-captains had been huddling.

"Listen up Quaker candidates!" Kara yelled. "We had such a good time watching your performances last night, that we want you to do it again. On the last night of tryouts, we'll ask you to entertain this whole group, again, as though it were halftime at a basketball game. After that, the co-captains and Ms. Dunflap, will meet to select our next Quaker – and the rest of the cheerleading squad for next year."

That night, I did not sleep well. I felt so good about my initial performance, but now I had to come up with another one. I had no idea what I would do. The idea for the first skit hit me like a bolt from the blue. "What happens if lightning doesn't strike twice?" I said out loud to myself. "Think, think, think – or maybe forget about it for a while and see what happens."

And that's what I did. For the next few days, I went to classes, went to cheerleading practice, spent time with my housemates and studied. Then one morning while standing in the shower, cascading warm water rinsing the shampoo from my hair, it dawned on me.

Again, there was a flurry of activity. Again, I gathered the props I would need. This time they included a large trunk, borrowed from my housemate Lowell,[7] an old steel mop bucket with a set of heavy-duty wheels on the bottom that we used to clean the kitchen floor, red, orange, and yellow construction paper, the cardboard center of a paper towel roll, an empty plastic gallon milk container, an empty tennis ball can, and, of course, my trusty friend the rubber chicken. I bought more poster board and wrote out the signs I would need – all the while envisioning what I would be doing as those signs were revealed to the crowd. As I finished writing the last sign, I felt myself once again brimming with optimism.

The last night of tryouts couldn't come fast enough. When it did, I dragged the trunk with all the other props in it through campus and down to the Palestra. Once inside, I asked Laura if she'd be my assistant again, and she readily agreed.

The nervous energy running through the gym was palpable. This was it! Everyone knew this was the last chance to impress the judges and make the squad. One by one, all the cheerleader

---

[7] Lowell is my oldest childhood friend with whom I still maintain contact. We first met when we were six-year-old first graders at a Chanukah party in the basement of an old church in Newington, Connecticut that served as a synagogue for our newly formed Jewish congregation while it built its own building across town. Lowell had just moved to town with his family from New York and was clearly uncomfortable in his new surroundings. His dad encouraged him to eat some latkes and apple sauce like "this boy here." "This boy here" was me as I was sitting across from Lowell and his father. We struck up a conversation and became fast friends.

candidates – Quaker finalists, too - had to perform the cheers complete with the appropriate moves. The judges, all seated together in the stands about six rows up from the floor and slightly to the left side as we faced them, were looking for proper arm angles and precise movements as they scratched notes on their clipboards rating each person's performance. Once everyone had finished, Steve directed us to take a seat in the stands in the first few rows. He announced, "Now we get to watch our Quaker candidates perform."

I was too excited to watch the other candidates perform their routines. Instead, I kept repeatedly reviewing in my mind what I needed to do when my turn came. And when it did, I sprang into action. I dragged the borrowed trunk out to center court, positioned it between the crowd and me, opened it, and left the lid up while I removed most of the props to shield them from the crowd's view and placed them on the floor beside me to keep them hidden.

I motioned for Laura to come join me, positioned her about six feet to the left of the trunk and laid the poster board signs facedown at her feet. Once I returned to my position standing behind the trunk, Laura bent down and raised the first sign, which read, "Welcome to the Quaker's School of Cooking." With that, I reached into the trunk, pulled out and put on a white apron and a chef's hat I borrowed from the university dining service. At the sight of me in chef's attire, co-captain/judge Steve, burst out laughing. "We're off to a good start," I thought to myself and closed the trunk.

The next sign read, "First, we need to put a pot on the stove." In response, I lifted the mop bucket onto the trunk. "Add water and light the stove," read the next one. I emptied the gallon jug, which I had filled part way with water into the bucket. Then I reached down, picked up the cardboard paper towel roll onto which I had taped a large wad of red construction paper and, with a big motion of my arm, struck the "giant match" against the sole of my shoe. I took the "lit" match and placed it against the bottom of the bucket. I turned the bucket around revealing to the crowd red, orange, and yellow flames (the construction paper I had cut into jagged pieces and taped to the bucket). The crowd laughed and we were cooking!

Laura raised the sign that read "Add chopped celery." I grabbed a celery stalk and a large kitchen knife and began chopping the celery high in the air above the pot. It was flying everywhere! Some may have even made it into the pot. The crowd was laughing, but, out of the corner of my eye, I noticed that Steve had turned away. He was no longer watching. "Uh oh!" I thought, "That's not good, but we have to keep going."

"Next add chopped carrots," read the next sign. Again, I chopped a whole bunch high above the pot continuing to make a vegetable mess all around me.

The next sign said, "Now add some pepper and stir." I grabbed the tennis can, which I had completely wrapped in a sheet of white paper, and on which was written in large black letters "P-E-P-P-E-R," and began shaking it over the pot. After a few seconds, I leaned my head back slightly and unleashed a very loud "ACHOO!" that sent my chef's hat flying over the pot to the other side of the trunk. The crowd laughed at the slapstick move as I ran to retrieve my hat.

Once I returned to my position behind the trunk and began stirring the pot with a ladle, Laura lifted the next sign that read, "Now the question is: What has the Quaker cooked?" As Laura reached for the last sign, I reached into the pot. Simultaneously, she revealed the sign, "Princeton's goose!" while I shot my arm out of the pot grasping the rubber chicken (which I had secretly placed in the pot ahead of time) by the neck and held it high above my head to the hearty applause and shouts of the assembled crowd. Steve, however, was still not looking.

Chapter 4 – The Call, the Result, and the Explanation

Tryout over, I went home to await the results. Arriving around 8:30, I was greeted by some of my housemates who asked me how it went. I told them I felt good about my performance, but also felt a twinge of doubt as one of the co-captains had basically ignored my performance. We just had to wait.

And wait we did. Nine o'clock, nine-thirty, ten o'clock. Still no word. I brought the hallway phone with the long cord (we only had a landline in those days) into my second-floor bedroom.

"Are you sure, you'll hear tonight?" a deep voice called down from the third floor. It was Mike whose booming voice led us to nickname him G-d.

"That's what they told us. They said they'd be calling everyone tonight," I yelled back.

The wait continued. Ten-thirty. Ten forty-five. Brrrrrrrrrrrring! I snatched up the phone.

"Hello," I said heart pounding.

"Brian?" the feminine voice on the other end asked.

"Yes."

"It's Kara. I'm calling to congratulate you. You're the Quaker!"

"Thank you," I said quietly.

"Is that it?" she asked incredulously. "I just had to make eleven other phone calls telling people they didn't get it and that's the only reaction I'm going to get out of you?!"

"Hold on," I told her. Pulling the phone away from my mouth, "I'M THE QUAKER!!!" I excitedly screamed to my housemates. "WOOOOHOOO!!!"

Putting the phone back near my mouth, I asked "Is that better, Kara?" as my housemates came running to congratulate me.

"Much!" she said. "Glad to hear you're excited! Steve and I are, too."

"Well thank you very much Kara, I am excited and look forward to working with you. See you soon. Gotta go now."

As I hung up the phone, my housemate, Dave, said, "O.k., that's it. We have to go out and celebrate!"

We put on our jackets and walked to a nearby bar. To anyone who would listen, Dave excitedly told him or her that I had just been selected as the next Penn Quaker. I think Dave took special pride in that accomplishment as he certainly had played an important role. If it weren't for him, I might never have gone to Penn.

I had known Dave since we were chemistry lab partners at William H. Hall High School (Hall High) in West Hartford, Connecticut. He was a senior and I was a junior. One day, Dave walked in and told me he had just gotten into the University of Pennsylvania. I congratulated him but had no idea why that was such a big deal. In my mind, Dave was a really smart guy. What I couldn't understand was if Dave wanted to go to a state school, why didn't he pick UConn. Something just didn't compute.

Later that day, I went to the resource room in the library and looked up the University of Pennsylvania in the Barron's Profiles of American Colleges. That's when I learned that the University of Pennsylvania (UPenn or Penn for short) was <u>not</u> a state school. Rather it was a member of the Ivy League. The next day when I walked into chemistry class, I told Dave that when he got to Penn, I'd love to come visit him.

Dave remembered that conversation and, when he got to Penn, he invited me to visit him that October. Dave met me as my train arrived at 30th Street Station on a Thursday night. It was my first time in Philadelphia.

As we emerged from the west side of the train station, Dave stopped and pointed to the partially obscured huge neon sign on the side of a building about a block away and smartly quipped, "That just about sums it up!" At that moment, the visible part of the sign read, "Bull." We laughed. As we continued walking, the rest of the sign came into view. "Bulletin" was the complete message. The building to which it was attached, I learned, was the home of The Philadelphia Bulletin, then the city's evening newspaper (unfortunately, like many papers, it no longer exists).

Dave and I walked the few blocks through the city to the Penn campus passing Drexel University on the way. As we strode through Penn's campus, he pointed out different buildings illuminated by floodlights – among them Hillhouse, the Fine Arts Library, Van Pelt Library, and College Hall. As we turned left down a wide path in the center of campus the patinaed copper gothic towers of the Quad's front gate came into view. At that very moment, I felt a twinge in my gut. It was love at first sight. I knew then and there that this was the place I wanted to go to school.

The main gate of the Quad that gave me that "gut" feeling that this was the place for me.
Photo courtesy of Adam Smith

And now here we were, three and a half years later celebrating my "mascothood." After a couple of cold drinks, we headed home. I was quite happy.

Falling asleep that night proved difficult, however, as the realization of what had happened sunk in and an electric feeling flowed through my body. I was the Quaker! WOW!

The next morning, I headed to class through an area of campus known as Superblock. Superblock consisted of three high-rise dorms for upper classmen arranged in a configuration that created a wind tunnel making it very uncomfortable to walk through when it was cold outside. On this particular day, however, the sun was shining brightly, and the temperature was warm when I happened upon cheerleading co-captain Steve coming in the opposite direction. He smiled broadly as he saw me and raised his right hand over his head. We high-fived.

"Congratulations, man! You deserved it!" Steve said.

"Thanks, Steve. I'm really excited! But there's one thing I don't understand."

Steve cocked his head to the side and looked at me questioningly.

"How could you have picked me when you weren't even watching me last night?"

"No, you don't understand," Steve explained. "I COULDN"T watch you. After I laughed so hard at your first skit about the basketball clinic, the other judges told me I wasn't being fair to the other finalists – that I had to tone it down. And then last night, as soon as you put on that chef's hat, I immediately started losing it again. The only way I could stop myself from laughing hysterically was to bite hard on my tongue and turn away. It was just too funny!"

"Really?! That's incredible!" I had a huge smile as I felt my chest swell with pride and excitement. You're never really sure you're funny until you get people's reactions. Steve's glowing comments gave me a huge confidence boost. "Well, I certainly hope I won't let you down."

You won't," Steve replied as we headed our separate ways.

Chapter 5 – Juggling and a Real Quaker Meeting

A few days after getting "the call," the annual Penn tradition "Spring Fling" began. Spring Fling is a huge multi-day campus-wide festival with lots of food, music, games, and drinking. Did I mention the drinking? Kegs, cases, flasks, pretty much any type of container that can hold liquid could be found everywhere. Most of the activities took place in the Quad.

Walking through the Quad with my friends, Lowell, John, Todd, and Bruce, I had many offers of liquid refreshments from people I just met after they learned from my friends that I was going to be the Quaker in the fall. Oh, and my friends benefited from people's largesse as well (except for Lowell who was not a drinker, but kept an eye out for the rest of us).

During one round of random wandering, I came upon a table hosted by the Penn Juggling Club. For five bucks they had a starter juggling set composed of three weighted tennis balls. A small hole had been cut into each ball, which was then filled with lead shot. The purpose was to deaden any bounce making it easier to work with the balls while learning to juggle. Thinking that juggling might be a useful skill to have as the Quaker, I bought a set. The club member who made the sale also gave me some basic instructions on how to juggle and helpful beginner's tips (such as practicing over a bed to make picking up the dropped balls easier). From that day on, I practiced daily and eventually could do some basic juggling.

Suddenly, out of nowhere, this lithe blonde woman came running at me and threw her arms around me. It was Brooke, now a Penn alumna who was living in the Philly area. As perky as ever, Brooke beamed at me.

"Congratulations, Brian! I heard the great news! The Quaker! Wow! That's fantastic and you deserve it. I am proud of you and proud to know you," she gushed.

"Thanks, Brooke! I'm thrilled. And if it weren't for you coming around the dorm last year, I wouldn't be the Quaker," I replied smiling back at her.

Brooke said, "Ya know, Brian, I could take you to a Quaker meeting if you're interested in seeing what real Quakers are about."

"You can?"

"Yeah, I belong to the Quaker Meeting House downtown."

"You do? I had no idea. I'd love to go with you to see what it's like. It could only help me in my new role."

And with that, we made a date to go to the Quaker meeting Sunday morning at 10.

When Sunday rolled around, I was excited and a little nervous as I had never experienced a Quaker meeting and didn't know what to expect. I also did not want to do anything out of my ignorance of the religion and its customs that might inadvertently offend someone and embarrass Brooke. Brooke picked me up at my off-campus house a little before ten. In the car on the way to the meeting I confessed my apprehension to her.

"Don't worry," Brooke assured me. She gave me a brief explanation of what I was about to witness. It went almost exactly as she described it.

We went into the Quaker Meeting House and took a seat in a pew to the right of the altar upon which the elders sat. The center pews faced the altar. The pews on either side faced the center pews. Everyone sat silently. As Brooke had explained to me, Quakers meditate at the meeting and stand and speak only if the spirit moves them. On this morning, apparently no one was moved. There was just dead silence. It was very relaxing.

After nearly an hour, one elder on the altar turned to another, extended his right hand, and said, "Good morning!" At this point, everyone in the room rose from his or her seat and slowly turned 360 degrees greeting each person who was close by with a hearty "Good morning!" and a handshake. Then everyone sat down again.

The elder who first broke the silence then asked if there were any guests in the house. A few different members rose to introduce individuals they had brought with them followed by a brief word or two from each of the guests.

Brooke stood, turned towards me with arms extended, and said, "I have brought Brian Becker with me. He's going to be the Penn Quaker and wanted to see what real Quakers did at a meeting."

The congregants laughed.   And the elder said, "Welcome!" as he motioned for me to stand up and invited me to speak.

"I'm happy to be here. Thank you for letting me be a part of your morning," I said and sat back down next to Brooke.

After a few general announcements, the meeting was over, and we moved to another room where refreshments were served. Following some light banter with several congregants, Brooke and I left the Meeting House and she drove me home.

"What did ya think?" Brooke asked as we pulled out of the parking lot.

"Just like you said," I replied. "Very interesting. It was a great experience. Thanks for inviting me."

"My pleasure," said Brooke. We rode the rest of the way back to my place in relative quiet. Brooke dropped me off and we said our goodbyes.

The rest of the semester went by quickly. In addition to catching up on my reading and studying for exams, I also got to celebrate becoming a senior with the rest of my class on "Hey Day" – a Penn tradition marking the advancement of the classes. On Hey Day, the junior class marches around campus in festive shirts and "straw" (Styrofoam) skimmer hats while carrying bamboo canes and plenty of booze!   All through the march, classmates take bites out of each other's hats. When the procession reaches College Hall, everyone forms an archway with the canes. The University President is escorted through the archway by the class officers.   Upon emerging from the archway, the President officially declares the junior class "seniors" and all hell breaks loose. It's great fun!

Celebrating "Hey Day" with my classmates shortly after being chosen as the next Penn Quaker.
Photo from author's personal photo collection

Following closely on the heels of Hey Day were finals. After exams I returned to Connecticut and my summer job cleaning and patrolling the beaches of Neptune Park, a private beach association in New London. One day while practicing my juggling on the beach, a longtime member of Neptune Park came up to me and taught me a few tricks to add some pizzazz to my juggling performance including a real showstopper - the Handless Catch and Toss Trick. The Handless Catch and Toss Trick involved catching a ball on the back of my neck and flipping it back into the air with my head to keep the juggling rhythm going without missing a beat. This trick proved to be particularly useful in a couple of instances. More on that later.

Chapter 6 – Cheerleading Camp

In early August, I took time off from my summer job to join the rest of the newly minted 1983-1984 Penn cheerleading squad in Philadelphia. There the 13 of us, 7 men and six women, loaded into a van and traveled to the campus of Virginia Tech in Blacksburg, Virginia, home of the Hokies. It was also the location for the Universal Cheerleading Association Spirit Camp. I admit I was somewhat skeptical of the notion of cheerleading camp. I had no idea what to expect, but thought, "What the heck, at least there'd be lots of pretty girls." Little did I know just how many!

After six and a half hours in the van, we arrived at our destination mid-afternoon. Blacksburg in August is a sauna – even worse than Philadelphia! As soon as we got out of the van, we were hot and sticky. We moved our stuff into the un-air-conditioned dorm rooms where we would be staying and then joined the seventy other cheerleading squads from around the eastern half of the country in a wide-open field outside the dorms.

The sun beat down and the humidity was thick. There was a stage set up on one end of the field that had a microphone at its center and two large speakers on either end. Some administrators were fussing with the microphone as we moved in their general direction. As I looked around, I couldn't help but notice the squads from Vanderbilt and VCU whose female members all had beautiful long blonde hair paired with long tanned legs. Wow!

"Testing 1,2,3, testing," the man at the microphone spoke into it. "Can everyone hear me?"

"Yes!" yelled the crowd as heads nodded up and down.

"Welcome to the Universal Cheerleading Association Spirit Camp. I am the director, Ron, and on behalf of my staff and myself, we hope you are going to have a great time this week as we help you develop and hone your skills so that you can really wow them when you return home. We'll be conducting morning and afternoon sessions each day. The morning sessions will begin at 9 a.m. Breakfast will be available at the dining hall beginning at 8 a.m."

The crowd groaned a little bit. "A little early for you?" asked Ron laughing. He resumed, "At least it should be a little cooler then. We'll work on drills in the morning, take a break for lunch from 12-2 and then work on stunts in the afternoon until about 5. After that, you'll have about an hour to rest and get cleaned up before dinner in the dining hall at 6. You're free to do whatever you like after dinner except on our last night when we'll have some special entertainment – more on that later in the week."

"That's the schedule for most of you," Ron continued. "And then there are our mascots. You guys will be off on your own led by two experienced hands – Johnny Reb from Ole Miss and the Wake Forest Deacon. You'll be meeting at the same times as the cheerleading squads but will take all your directions from them – and that starts right now. So come on down to just in front of the stage and once you're all here you'll head off with them."

"See you later guys," I said to my fellow Penn cheerleaders as I made my way toward the stage. I saw others making their way toward the stage, too. In just a couple of minutes fifty mascots had gathered and we marched off with Johnny Reb and the Deacon toward a low-rise brick building. We went inside and entered a large, dimly lit, but otherwise non-descript, square room. The size and shape of it reminded me a little bit of my high school band room. The best part about being in the room was that it was significantly cooler inside than it was in the sweltering heat out on the field.

"Have a seat everybody," said Johnny Reb. "Welcome to mascot training. This is where we'll be meeting each day."

As everyone settled down on the floor, the Deacon picked up where Johnny Reb had left off. "We're gonna teach you all about the 'Mascot Code' and forever change the way you think about being a mascot," he said. "But first, let's find out who's here. We'll go around the room and have everyone introduce himself. When I point at you, please stand up, tell us what school you are from and what your school's mascot is."

One by one, we took turns standing up giving the requested information. When my turn came, I stood, smiled nervously, looked around the room and said, "Hi, I'm Brian from the University of Pennsylvania and I'm the Quaker." Then I quickly sat down. Among those in attendance were the Ohio State Buckeye, the Penn State Nittany Lion, the Syracuse Orange, the Florida Gator, the Vanderbilt Commodore, and the Northwestern Wildcat.

Once we'd all introduced ourselves, our instructors gave us their backgrounds. Each was about to begin his third year as his school's mascot and had learned a lot along the way including the importance of the Mascot Code.

"The Mascot Code," the Deacon stated, "is the most important thing we can impart to you during our few days together. It is what makes being a mascot special and is what gives you the freedom to let it all hang out."

"That's right," Johnny Reb chimed in. "It forms the foundation of everything we do. So, what exactly is the Mascot Code?"

That's what each of us wanted to know as we looked at each other and, collectively, shrugged our shoulders. Our curiosity piqued; the group leaned forward in anticipation.

"The Mascot Code is a series of principles that govern our thoughts and actions as mascots – what we should do as well as what we shouldn't do," Johnny Reb continued. "And first among those principles is 'Mascots are INFALLIBLE!' What's that you say? How could that be? Well, it's true. When you don your costume, you are infallible."

"Huh?" I thought while asking myself the very same questions Johnny Reb had just posed. We all continued listening intently to our leaders.

"There has never been a mascot that has made a mistake. If you make a mistake, you MEANT to make it," Johnny Reb stated. "If you trip, go back and do it again in slow motion. You can always make something seem as though you intended to do it even if you hadn't intended to do it. People will never know the difference."

"Now the next thing you want to do," said the Deacon, "is decide what type of character you want your mascot to be and then develop that character. Do you want your character to be strong and bold taking large steady steps along the sidelines or do you want it to be a zany character running around in circles and jumping up and down like it has ants in its pants? Some of that decision may be made for you by your costume. If your costume has a large head and large feet, it is a lot harder to run around. And keep in mind you need to stay in character the entire time you are in costume, which will be hours at a time. So, whatever you come up with must be something you can sustain over a long period of time. That is what we will be spending the lion's share of our time doing this week – helping you work on developing and refining your character."

"And while developing your character, you should keep in mind certain other mascot rules, "said Johnny Reb. "For instance, mascots whose costumes include large heads, which is most of you, should never speak. It ruins the aura of your larger-than-life character. Also, and I mean this seriously, you should NEVER take your head off in public. I saw this happen once and a bunch of little kids went into a panic. They were screaming and crying. Now, you certainly don't want to be the cause of that!"

Amid the many heads nodding up and down, there were a few nervous chuckles.

"Now mascots without costume heads have certain advantages and disadvantages," he continued. "You can speak, but you need to speak in character. You can use facial expressions, but you must remember that from afar people may not be able to see them well. And most of you without costume heads also lack the extra-large hands and feet that usually come with the costumes of those with heads. Therefore, you need to work on exaggerating all your motions so that you appear to be bigger than life. Remember you will be performing before tens of thousands of people, and you want all of them to be able to tell what you are doing.”

“Another thing that is extremely important to keep in mind,” added the Deacon, “is that you are your school’s representative. Whatever you do reflects on your entire school. Also, because you are your school’s representative, you should <u>never</u> fight with another mascot as you could incite a riot in the crowd as others from each school could follow your lead.”

“It’s happened. That’s a true statement,” he continued in response to the incredulous looks and headshaking around the room. “Not to mention you also could damage your costume and the costume of the other mascot – and these things aren’t cheap. So please keep this advice in mind. It’s imperative. Good-natured teasing or chasing each other around is one thing, but fighting is a definite ‘no-no’.”

“Yet another thing that is imperative has to do with your safety,” said Johnny Reb.

“What?” I thought to myself. “Safety? What do you mean our safety?”

“As a mascot, people will always be thinking you’re just goofing around and that your actions are not to be taken seriously. So, if you were to get injured, you need to be able to signal to someone that your injury is real and that you need help. You should always have at least one member of your cheerleading squad – someone you trust – keep an eye on you and come to your assistance should you need it. You'll also want to develop a sign that you can use to summon help from that person – especially those of you whose costumes will not allow you to speak."

"Now we're going to have you pair up and work with your partner to develop your mascot's character. For purposes of this camp, your partner and each of us," Johnny Reb said while pointing to himself and then at the Deacon, "will serve as your 'handlers' and keep an eye out in case you get into real trouble."

"We happen to have an even number of you, which is good," observed the Deacon. "That means that everyone will have a partner. Let's have you pair up now. Just pick the person sitting closest to you."

With that, everyone turned one way or another until everyone had a partner. I turned to my left and shook hands with Bill, the Vanderbilt Commodore. Bill was about six foot three with blonde hair, blue eyes, and a large, stocky build. As my mother would say, he had "big bones." Bill reminded me a little bit of my best friend from high school, Andy, a tuba player.

"Now that you have your partner, we're going to go over our general schedule for the week and then call it a day as it is now just about five," said the Deacon. "Think about what we told you today and start thinking about your character tonight. Then we'll meet back here in the morning and get to work."

"As Ron said in the field earlier today, the Deacon continued, "the cheerleading squads will be working on the field from 9-12 in the mornings and 2-5 in the afternoons. We'll be doing the same, except our morning sessions will be in here as we work on different aspects of being a mascot and then after lunch, we'll have you get dressed in your costumes and set you loose to practice your craft among the cheerleading squads during the afternoon sessions."

"Wait. What did he just say?" I asked myself. I turned to Bill and asked, "Did he just say we'll be wearing our costumes in the afternoons?"

"Yes," replied Bill.

"Do you have your costume here?" I asked.

"Sure do," said Bill. Looking at the consternation on my face, he asked, "You mean you don't?"

"Nope. I haven't even gotten it yet. I had no idea that I would need it for this. Nobody told me."

Bill shook his head from side-to-side empathizing with my plight. "What are you going to do?" he asked.

"Not sure."

"O.k. everybody, have a great night," said Johnny Reb to the group.

As everyone was filing out of the room, I approached the Deacon and explained my predicament. It would be kind of tough for me to go out among the cheerleading squads each afternoon playing the Quaker while wearing only a t-shirt and shorts. People would have no idea what I was doing and would probably think I was a cheerleader who had gone AWOL from his squad and lost his mind.

The Deacon called Johnny Reb over to confer and the two of them took me to see Ron to ask his advice. Ron, being a local, said there was a thrift shop nearby and that perhaps I could cobble together a costume with some things I could find there. I thanked Ron for the suggestion and the directions to the thrift shop he gave me, and then went in search of co-captain Steve who had the keys to the van in which we'd driven to camp.

I rushed up to Steve upon seeing him and asked, "Guess what?"

"What?" Steve said with a smile.

"Apparently I need my costume and I don't have it!" I said with a strong note of annoyance in my voice.

The smile dropped off Steve's face. "Sorry man," he said. "What are you going to do?"

"I'm going to try to make some semblance of a Quaker costume, but I need to go to a thrift shop they have here in town to see what I can find. I need to borrow the van."

"O.k.," said Steve. "And I'll come with you."

We hopped in the van, Steve at the wheel. Riding shotgun I read the directions and about ten minutes later we parked in front of the Blacksburg thrift shop, cleverly named "The Thrift Shop." It was small and dimly lit with all sorts of items stacked in piles on tables throughout the store. After rummaging through the merchandise for twenty minutes or so, I happened upon a black tricorn hat with a $10 price tag on it. I put it on my head and called to Steve who was on the opposite side of the store. He smiled. "That'll work!" he said as he swung his head in a slight scoop to the right. After several more minutes of fruitless searching, I paid for the hat, and Steve and I headed back to camp.

We got back just in time for dinner. Fried chicken, mashed potatoes and gravy, corn on the cob and salad were served family style on long tables. While you could sit anywhere, most people sat with their own squads and ate rather quietly as everyone was tired from the travel, the heat, and the day's activities.

After dinner, I went up to one of the administrators and asked if there was any plain white paper, blue paper, a pair of scissors, some scotch tape, and some masking tape I could use. Within a few minutes she had managed to find everything. I thanked her and headed back to my dorm room.

I looked through the army duffel bag I had brought with me and pulled out a Penn t-shirt, a pair of dark blue sweatpants and a light blue, lightweight outdoor jacket I had brought with me just in case it got chilly. Then I began cutting the white paper into strips roughly three to four inches long and about a half an inch wide. Using the edge of the scissors, I curled each of the strips and scotch taped each strip onto one side of a piece of blue paper in rows across the page until I had about twenty rows starting three or four inches from the top and running down the entire page. Then I applied masking tape in numerous spots on the reverse side of the paper and attached it at the top of the front side of my Penn t-shirt, trimming the upper edge of the paper into a curve so that it would sit just below the neckline of the t-shirt. What an oddity – a t-shirt with frills!

I carefully tried on the shirt and then slipped on the jacket zipping it up just enough to cover any part of the t-shirt not covered with the paper jabot I had created. I put on the sweatpants and pulled the legs up to the top of my high white socks to make the pants look like knickers. I put on the tricorn hat and made my way to the full-length mirror on the back of the dorm door. Looking at the reflection, I thought it was a very rough, but reasonable facsimile of my costume. It wasn't great, but hey, it was better than nothing and at least people could assume I was a mascot rather than a demented cheerleader made insane by the heat.

I gently undressed trying to avoid destroying the paper jabot and lost only a few strips in the process. I picked them up, reattached them and then gently placed the shirt down on top of a dresser. Exhausted, I fell into bed and fell asleep despite the uncomfortably warm humid night air hanging in the room.

I woke up the next morning, as the sunshine streamed through the uncovered window of the dorm room, thinking about the type of character the Quaker should be - strong and bold, or zany, or something else completely? I thought back on my tryout skits and how I would need to appear before large crowds and decided that zany it would be.

 Arriving in the mascot training room after breakfast, I joined Bill in the middle of the floor and engaged in small talk while awaiting our instructors. A few minutes later, in came the Deacon and Johnny Reb.

"Good morning!" chirped the Deacon as Johnny Reb gave us a wave. "As we said yesterday, today you will work with your partner on creating and honing your mascot's character. Johnny Reb and I also will walk around to see what you're up to and to offer suggestions from time to time. So, let's get started."

With that, Bill and I traded our ideas for our mascot characters. Bill said he thought his character, the Commodore, should be big and bold. His costume and his size made that a good fit. He demonstrated how he thought he should strut around moving his arms very deliberating in wide, slow swings and turning his head slowly from side to side. When he stopped, he put his fisted hands on his hips and puffed out his chest. Looked good to me.

Then it was my turn. With Johnny Reb joining us at that point, I explained that I wanted to make the Quaker a zany character. With that, I walked quickly back and forth, almost like a power walker, and occasionally flung my arms into the air and jumped. I had never done anything like this before and it showed. Johnny Reb reminded me that because my costume did not have the features to instantly create a bigger-than-life character, I needed to over-exaggerate my motions. He suggested swinging my arms from side to side as I walked. I tried his suggestion pushing my elbows out from my body.

"Bigger!" he encouraged. "Faster!"

I raised my elbows alternately as high as I could get them to go in rhythm with my quick, short-stride, stiff-paced walk. And the "Quaker-walk" was born.

"That's good." Johnny Reb said. "Keep working on it." After checking out Bill's walk and actions and making a couple of suggestions, Johnny Reb moved on to the next group.

Bill and I continued alternating acting in character and watching and critiquing one another. We'd point out when the other fell out of character and encouraged each other when things were going well. After a couple of hours, Johnny Reb and the Deacon asked everyone to grab some water and take a seat.

"Good work everybody," said the Deacon. "You all appear to be making some good progress. Things are really coming along."

"Now this afternoon," he continued, "we're going to have you get into your costumes for the first time and go out among the cheerleading squads to continue practicing what you have been doing this morning."

"But before we break for lunch," said Johnny Reb, "the Deacon and I thought we'd share some more thoughts with you about the mascot mindset that you can use while practicing. Specifically, you should always be on the lookout for opportunities to interact with people and the general environment. Pay attention to what's going on around you and use your creativity to incorporate it into your act."

"For example," he continued, "something as simple as walking up behind a security guard and then mimicking his motions works wonderfully. The crowd really gets into it when the security guard gets more and more confused as more and more people focus on him for what, to him, appears to be no apparent reason. When he eventually discovers what's going on, you can good-naturedly shake his hand and be off and running."

"Or everyone likes to pick on referees," added the Deacon. "This is particularly good to do at away games where you might not have that many fans from your own school in the crowd. Even the other side's fans can get into you picking on the refs."

Our entire group was enthralled with the stories Johnny Reb and the Deacon shared. Useful advice, spoken from real experience I thought as I continued soaking it all in.

"Now after lunch," concluded the Deacon, "you should return here with your costumes. We'll all get into our costumes and then go out into the field to play for a couple of hours. Keep in mind that it is really hot out there so be sure to hydrate well during lunch."

Off we went into the summer steam bath. We drank as much water as humanly possible at lunch, heeding the Deacon's advice. Then it was back to the oven-like dorm rooms to grab our uniforms.

I brought my olive-green army bag holding the makeshift costume and weighted tennis balls back to the mascot's training room. Arriving a few minutes ahead of schedule, I decided to relax a little bit by practicing my juggling. A few of the other mascots scattered about the room watched. After I did the trick of catching the ball on the back of my neck and tossing it back into the air with my head, Ryan, the Northwestern Wildcat, approached me.

"Hey that was cool!" he said. "My big stunt is to get rammed into the goalposts spread eagle after each Northwestern score without getting hurt. I'll trade you that secret if you teach me how to do that trick."

"You get rammed into the goalposts spread eagle?" I said incredulously. "And you don't get hurt?"

"Yup."

"Do you wear a cup?"

"Nope."

"Really? You must nuts! Or you don't have any!" I joked.

"Nah. It's really not that hard," he said. Do we have a deal?"

"Sure. Why not."

Ryan explained how his stunt was done. It was quite clever. Four cheerleaders would each grab a different limb and run him toward the goalpost with his legs stretched out to either side ramming him into the goalposts. There was a secret trick to performing the stunt without getting hurt. With the one special exception (described below), I never shared the secret of that trick with anyone but the cheerleaders who assisted me – not even my wife. I would share it with you now, but I can't.

You see, when my kids were young, I told them this story. I also told them that no matter how much they pleaded with me, I wouldn't tell them the secret unless … they got into Penn and enrolled (I figured this would give them something to shoot for and perhaps one of them might someday become the Quaker during his time there). Long story short, my older son, Casey, actually did go to Penn and I did reveal the secret to him. While writing this book, I thought about sharing the secret with you, but Casey objected saying he had worked hard to earn the right to know. So, in fairness to him, I won't reveal how the stunt was done here. If you want to know, you'll just have to ask Casey!

Now, back to where we were in our story. After learning about the goalpost routine, I decided this was something I could really use! The Wildcat and I then spent the remaining time before our instructors returned with me teaching him how to do The Handless Catch and Toss Trick I had learned at the beach. He almost got it by the time Johnny Reb and the Deacon walked in carrying their own costumes.

"O.k. everybody," announced the Deacon, "time to get dressed."

People around the room began pulling out their costumes and climbing into them. I reached into my bag and gently removed my t-shirt with the paper frills that I had handcrafted the night before. Once again, I delicately constructed my costume – t-shirt slowly lowered over my head and pulled into place, jacket placed over the t-shirt and zipped up just enough to hide the areas without the curled paper attached, sweatpants with the legs pulled up to my knees, and tricorn hat pulled down on top of my head. Voila! The Quaker was raring to go!

"Now remember it's hot out there," cautioned Johnny Reb. "If during our time on the field, you feel the need for a drink, come back in here to get one. Remember, you should never remove your head in public."

Of course, this last piece of advice did not apply to me. Just like I was allowed to speak when in character, I could also have a drink. This made my life a lot easier, particularly in the sweltering heat.

"Now let's go have some fun!" Johnny Reb said before putting on his costume's head. He and the Deacon then led the way out onto the field. A parade of mascots followed behind.

The sun was shining brightly, and the heat and humidity were intense, but the excitement of bringing our characters out into the open for the first time pushed the uncomfortable conditions out of my mind as we made our way outside. I can only imagine what we must have looked like to the cheerleading squads who slowly turned to see the steady stream of mascots emerge onto the field.

With my newly developed Quaker-walk, I took brisk tiny steps with my arms swinging side to side. Walking first left, then right, then in a circle, then zigzagging, I searched for the Penn cheerleaders. Upon finding them, I made a beeline in their direction and proceeded to walk in wide circles around them. My teammates turned slowly, and their eyes followed me around and around. Suddenly I stopped, planted my hands on my hips, cocked my head and asked, "Well what do you think?" Steve's raucous laughter and the smiles and nods from the rest of the squad were all I needed to know that I had found a winning combination.

"Thanks guys! And now I'm off," I said with a nod, and began Quaker-walking around the field visiting (and flirting with) cheerleading squad after cheerleading squad, interacting with fellow mascots, and just having a good time – all while keeping in character. And so went the rest of cheerleading camp, with mascot training indoors in the mornings and the mascot posse hitting the field to wreak havoc in the afternoons. There were, however, two notable exceptions.

First, after dinner on the second-to-last night, most of the cheerleaders went off to a local bar with live music to have some fun. Walking in, the place was crowded and hot – in two ways: temperature and women! Everywhere you looked there were beautiful female cheerleaders. They were no longer looking grungy in sweats and t-shirts, but all cleaned up and dressed nicely in summer dresses, or blouses with short skirts or short shorts. And they all wanted to dance! In between dancing, we downed some cold beers. It was quite the night.

Second, on the last night of camp, the mascots were called up to perform. We had worked out a routine to a top country music hit, Swingin', by John Anderson - a song I had never heard of. The fact that I was unfamiliar with the song ordinarily wouldn't have mattered much except in this case it did. Why? Because as the only mascot in camp without a costume head, I was chosen to lip-sync the song while hopping around the stage as the other mascots acted out the actions in the song. Fortunately, we had practiced in our mascot room the last couple of mornings, so I had a chance to learn the lyrics, which are:

There's a little girl, in our neighborhood
Her name is Charlotte Johnson and she's really lookin' good.
I had to go and see her, so I called her on the phone.
I walked over to her house, and this was goin' on.

Her brother was on the sofa, eatin' chocolate pie.
Her momma was in the kitchen cuttin' chicken up to fry.
Her daddy was in the backyard rollin' up a garden hose.
I was on the porch with Charlotte feelin' love down to my toes,

And we were swingin' (swingin').
Yes, we were swingin' (swingin').
Little Charlotte she's as pretty as the angels when they sing.
I can't believe I'm out here on the front porch in the swing
Just a swingin' (swingin')
Just a swingin' (swingin')

Now Charlotte she's a darlin'. She's the apple of my eye.

When I'm on the swing with her it makes me almost high.
Now Charlotte is my lover and she has been since the spring.
I can't believe it started on her front porch in the swing.

And we were swingin' (swingin').
Yes, we were swingin' (swingin').
Little Charlotte she's as pretty as the angels when they sing.
I can't believe I'm out here on the front porch in the swing
Just a swingin' (swingin')
Just a swingin' (swingin')

It was a blast! And I think my performance on stage that night together with the playfulness in the field each afternoon in my makeshift costume earned me one of only a handful of "spirit sticks" handed out by Johnny Reb and the Deacon to those mascots who demonstrated the most spirit in camp. Here's a photo of the stick:

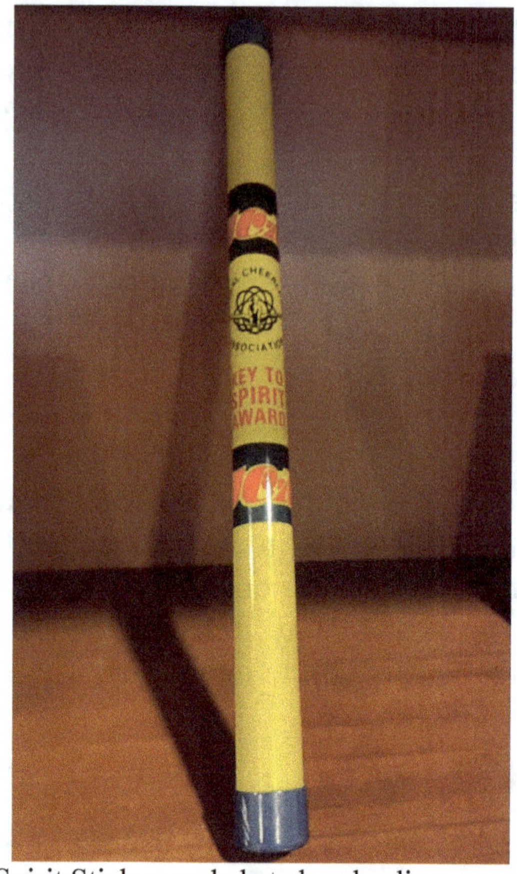

Spirit Stick awarded at cheerleading camp.
Photo from author's personal photo collection

At breakfast on the last morning, I said goodbye and good luck to my weeklong partner, Bill, and thanked Johnny Reb and the Deacon for all their good advice and help. Outside, I took one last look around. I shook my head slowly from side to side while admiring all the beautiful women, particularly those from the southern schools with long legs and blonde hair. Climbing into the van I marveled at all that I had seen and learned. Dozing off on the way back to Philadelphia I felt like I now had the tools to take the Quaker to the next level.

Chapter 7 – Picking Up the Costume and Prepping for Opening Night

Returning to school in early September, there was much to do in advance of the first football game of the season scheduled for Saturday night, September 17th. First, I had to get my official Quaker costume. Ms. Dunflap, in the Athletic Department, directed me to go to Pierre's Costumes on Walnut Street to get fitted and said she'd call ahead. A short time later, I walked into the small shop filled with various masks and costumes, I approached the counter and said, "Hi, I'm Brian Becker, the new Penn Quaker, and I'm here to get my costume fitted."

The gentleman behind the counter said, "Ah, yes, the Athletic Department called and said you would be coming by. My name is Ricard and I'll be helping you. Please step right over here." He directed me to a spot in front of a full-length mirror and then disappeared into a back room.

"Here we go," Ricard said as he emerged with the Quaker costume in hand. He laid it on a nearby table picked up the blue knickers and showed me how to adjust the waistband and the straps that would hold the pant legs just below my knees. Next, he handed me a white peasant shirt, a pair of long white socks and a pair of suspenders and directed me to the changing room.

I emerged from the dressing room clad in the pieces of the costume I had been given. I stepped back in front of the mirror and Ricard put the purplish waistcoat (akin to a tuxedo vest) over my head and fastened the strap behind my back. He grabbed a pure white jabot and expertly snapped it around my neck. Finally, he helped me put on the dark red coat. Looking back at me from the mirror was the Quaker. The sleeves of the coat, however, ended midway between my elbows and wrists, as the previous Quaker, Fred, had been much smaller than me. Ricard measured the difference between the end of each sleeve and each of my wrists and jotted down some notes. Then he abruptly said, "O.k., now go take it all off."

"Thank you," I replied, and quickly made my way back into the changing room. Once back in street clothes, I walked out of the changing room and placed the costume on the counter, asking Ricard, "When will it be ready?"

"Two days," he answered.

"Great. I'll be back then," I said, and headed off to my next stop, the Annenberg Center, which housed the Penn Band's practice room and office.

One of the things they impressed on us during mascot training was the importance of making a big entrance at our first home game. Traditionally, before the first home football game of the season, the Quaker was carried *sans* hat into Franklin Field lying stiffly, as though dead, on the shoulders of the male cheerleaders. They would put him down into a standing position and "hold him up" until his hat was placed upon his head at which time he would "come to life."

After investigating a few options – including parachuting into Franklin Field, which idea was shot down by the Athletic Department and Penn Security as too dangerous (probably a good thing as I had no skydiving or parachuting experience) – I settled on what I thought would be a memorable introduction for the Quaker. However, I needed the band's help - and permission to alter and use one piece of its equipment - to make the whole thing work. Hence, the meeting I had arranged with Claude, the Penn Band's staff director.

Arriving in the band's office, I found Claude rushing about pulling together papers from various piles about the room and creating a new pile. He stopped when he saw me and invited me to sit in a chair opposite the one he plopped himself down into on the other side of his cluttered desk.

Claude was around 40 and had tight curly brown hair, a high forehead, and horn-rimmed glasses. He was part composer, part arranger, part conductor, part musician, and had been leading the band for several years, including the first three years of my Penn career when I played alto sax (and kazoo) in the band.

"What can I do for you, Brian?" Claude asked. "Or should I say, Mr. Quaker?"

"Brian is fine, Claude." I said with a smile. "But I do have a few favors to ask of you."

"What are you looking for?"

"Well, I want to do something different for the Quaker's introduction this year and I'd like to alter and use the band's wooden drum as part of it." The band had a drum that stood about six and a half feet tall. It was on a set of wheels that enabled it to be wheeled into Franklin Field and onto the track encircling the football field ahead of the band as it marched into the stadium playing the University of Pennsylvania Band March.

"Go on," said Claude.

"My idea is sort of like the 'Trojan Quaker,'" I said. Claude raised his eyebrows as I continued.

"I know that Harvard defaced the drum last year by spray painting 'Harvard' on it. In exchange for me cleaning that slur off, I would like your permission to cut a door in one side of the drum so that I can ride inside it and jump out."

"Really!" Claude chuckled at the thought.

"And, favor number two, I'd like the band to help me out by playing Sprach Zarathustra [a/k/a the theme to 2001: A Space Odyssey] after the University of Pennsylvania Band March and before climbing into the stands. During the song, I'll have the cheerleaders rock the drum back and forth after the first two fanfares (while the timpani and base drums are playing) to make it look almost like an egg trying to hatch, and then I'll burst out of the drum after the third fanfare just as the band arrives at the majestic cadence – BA DAAAAAA!!! What do you think?"

"Sounds like a great idea! But do you really think you'll be able to get the drum cleaned up and cut a door into it without doing permanent damage to it?" Claude asked.

"The clean-up will be a pain and require a lot of elbow grease, but I know I can do it. The door not so much. I'm not very handy. I've talked to the maintenance staff, though, to get some help with it. I know my limitations," I said. "The maintenance staff told me they could cut a door that they could fasten with a couple of hinges at the bottom so that it would drop down like a ramp when released. After I use it, a couple of well-placed nails and a little touch-up paint should make the drum look almost as good as new – and certainly a lot better than it looks now with Hah-vahd painted on it."

"We'll do it!" said Claude with a quick nod.

"Thanks, I appreciate it! As part of this request, Claude, I would appreciate you not telling anyone – including the band about it. I know you'll have to rehearse the song with the band, and you'll have to instruct them in advance to remain on the track after finishing the University of Pennsylvania Band March to play the extra tune, but I would appreciate you not telling them the reason why. I am trying to keep this whole thing a surprise and the fewer people who know what's coming, the better."

"Got it. No problem. I think this'll be fun. Anything else?" he asked.

"Yeah. One more thing: following the extra point after Penn scores a touchdown, I'd like you to have the band do a drum roll and a cymbal crash before playing 'Hang Jeff Davis.' I won't tell you why right now, but you'll see. It's gonna be good," I said with a smile thinking this would be the perfect accompaniment to the new goalpost routine I was preparing to introduce.

"A little cryptic there. Huh, Brian?" Claude said with a wry smile.

I nodded and smiling back I said, "Yeah but I really appreciate your help."

"Anything for the Quaker who was one of ours first!" Claude said smiling fully now.

"Thanks, Claude," I said returning the smile and giving him a thumbs-up as I left his office.

In the days between my meeting with Claude and opening night, I continued my preparations. I bought paint remover and got some rags from the maintenance department and spent several hours scrubbing the band's drum clean and providing an extra set of hands for the skillful maintenance man who cut the door into the side of it. I picked up my costume at Pierre's and tried the whole outfit on when I got home. Lowell and John were there when I came downstairs wearing the outfit, so I asked them to take pictures of me as I stood atop the dining room table. Here's their handiwork:

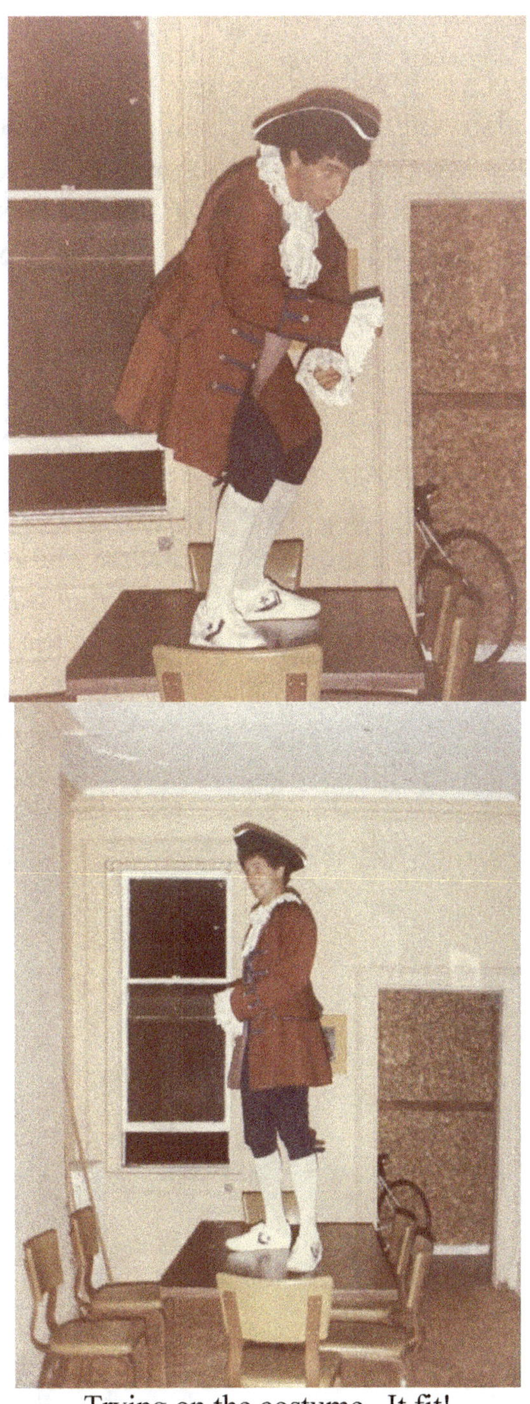

Trying on the costume. It fit!
Photos from author's personal photo collection

Of course, I also attended cheerleading practice, which ran about two hours two or three nights a week. I used some time at each practice to work with the male cheerleaders on the goalpost routine – particularly the all-important part about the secret to keep my child-producing options viable. Fortunately, they were fast learners!

Continuing to envision what I could do at the football games, I thought it might be a good idea to toss candy into the crowd at each game, so a couple of days before opening night, I bought some inexpensive hard candies at the Acme Market and stuffed full an old light green canvas book bag which a middle school friend's mom had made for me when I was in the sixth grade. I was ready!

Chapter 8 – Opening Night Nausea

One thing I haven't mentioned yet was that opening day posed a religious quandary for me. It fell on the tail end of Yom Kippur[8], which ran from sundown on Friday, September 16th, until sundown on Saturday the 17th. Jews fast during this holiday, which meant I had nothing to eat or drink (literally nothing, including water) for about twenty-five hours.

The game was not until evening, but it was still before sundown. While not exactly kosher, I compromised on my fast by starting it a little earlier on the day before and ending it just before I got dressed for the game. The result was that I did not have much time to digest my meal before having to take the field. For every other game, I would eat several hours before – just like the players – so enough time would pass before I had to head out to the field or the court.

After dressing in my costume, I had one more drink of water, grabbed the candy-stuffed canvas book bag, and headed off to the Annenberg Center where the cheerleading squad would gather to march with the band through campus down to Franklin Field. Arriving in the courtyard of the Annenberg Center in full costume, in character and doing the Quaker walk, several of my friends in the band started hooting and hollering.

---

[8] Yom Kippur is the "Day of Atonement" in the Jewish calendar.

Then one band member good-naturedly yelled, "The Quaker is a band jacket!" And that's all it took for the rest of the band to join in. "The Quaker is a band jacket! The Quaker is a band jacket!" This was an inside joke stemming from the fact that the year before, I had designed a band jacket for the Penn Band, collected money from band members, and placed the order with Champion. Then something went awry. Champion never produced the jackets. I ended up refunding everyone's money, but the fact that we never got the jackets obviously hadn't been forgotten.

As the heckling continued, I just shrugged my shoulders, shook my head, raised my palms up in the air and smiled. What else could I do? As the saying goes, no good deed goes unpunished. After another minute or two, I signaled enough already and then went over to the band and high-fived them before heading over to where the cheerleaders had set up next to a bench.

The band and cheerleaders got lined up. After four short blasts sounded from the drum major's whistle, the band's drummers started a street beat and off we went. We marched out of the courtyard and turned right down Locust Walk (the main walkway through the middle of campus). The band led the way with the cheerleaders following - all smiles, pom-poms waving. Arriving in Superblock, the drum major blew his whistle, the street beat came to an end and the band halted. The cheerleaders took up a position in front of High Rise East. The band played the school's fight song, "Fight On, Pennsylvania!" The cheerleaders (including yours truly) performed their well-rehearsed moves to the song – arms and pom-poms moving in rhythm - and students came out of the high-rise buildings to watch and listen. Upon concluding the fight song, the band played a pop tune from their repertoire and the cheerleaders built a human pyramid (while I acted as spotter for the cheerleader at the top).

Once the pop song had ended and the human pyramid had been disassembled, the drum major blew his whistle again and following his four sharp tweets, the snare drummers began hitting rim shots in march tempo and the band and cheerleaders were off again, back down Locust Walk, this time with many students from Superblock joining the parade. After sixteen rim shots, the bass drums joined in on the first beat of each measure and the band yelled out in rhythm, "'P', can't hear you. 'E,' little louder. 'N,' that's better. 'N,' now you got it! 'P', hit it! 'E,' hit it! 'N,' hit it! 'N,' hit it! P-E-N-N! P-E-N-N!" After which the rhythm section resumed the street beat as the parade marched on.

At 37th Street, the band took a right, and the parade went straight across Spruce Street halting traffic for several minutes as each member of the procession had to squeeze his or her way through the main gate of the Quad. Once through, the band and cheerleaders made their way to the Junior Balcony. The Junior Balcony provided a bird's eye view of the large open space inside the lower Quad.

Again, the band played the fight song. Again, the cheerleaders performed their moves. Again, students came out of the dorms to join the growing crowd. Again, the street beat began, and the band led the mass of humanity out the Quad gates and down all parts of Spruce Street toward Franklin Field.

When I say "all parts" of Spruce Street, that is exactly what I mean. The Penn Band liked to call itself the "Amorphous Penn Band" when it was marching down a street and this was with good reason. The outer columns of the band would peel off and veer toward the sidewalks, doing loops around parked cars, poles, pedestrians and anything or anyone else who happened to be ensnared in their unregulated and unrestrained marching path. Sometimes those columns would even go in and out of buildings always rejoining with the other columns that had continued marching down the middle of the street toward Franklin Field.

Arriving at the back entrance of Franklin Field, four cheerleaders grabbed the band's recently refurbished wooden drum, which I had arranged to be left just inside the entrance. I climbed into the drum. It was a tight fit inside. I had to stand on two-by-fours on either side of the door that had been cut for me, use one hand to hold the door closed and the other to help me maintain my balance – especially when the drum was moving. I had to be careful that I neither moved the door nor fell off a two-by-four and so as not to put my foot through the flimsy floor of the drum. The band began playing the University of Pennsylvania Band March and the cheerleaders started rolling the drum into the stadium and onto the track surrounding the football field.

En route, I was thinking how I had not accounted for my tricorn hat when the maintenance man and I had cut the door into the drum's side. I couldn't help but wonder whether I would lose it on the way out. I thought about holding it and stepping out carefully, but that would destroy the whole effect I was trying to achieve. I wanted it to appear that I burst through the side of the drum as though it were made of paper.

The band finished playing its march and the drum came to a halt. Then, just as Claude and I had discussed, the first notes of the theme to the movie 2001 A Space Odyssey sounded. "BAA, DAA, DAAAAAAA, BA DAAA!"   And then as the kettledrums and bass drums responded, "Bum-bum, bum-bum, bum-bum, bum-bum," the cheerleaders gripping the drum rocked it forward and back. That's when I really struggled to maintain my balance and keep the door closed. As the band started playing the second round of "BAA, DAA, DAAAAAA, BA DAAA!" I exhaled thinking I had survived round one.

Once again, as the kettledrums and bass drums responded, "Bum-bum, bum-bum, bum-bum, bum-bum," the cheerleaders gripping the drum rocked it forward and back. Again, I managed to hang on. Now it was time to get ready to come out. I decided to just go for it and hoped I didn't scalp myself in the process.

Again, "BAA, DAA, DAAAAAA," but this time on the last "BA DAAAAA!" I threw open the door and leapt through it in one motion as roaring applause broke out in the stands. Everyone was standing and applauding wildly. Seeing the crowd, I mistakenly figured the team must be running onto the field and immediately turned around to look. But there was no team yet. Laughter erupted from the crowd. As I turned back to look at them, it dawned on me that the applause had been for me and my grand entrance!

I, too, started laughing, and, if truth were told, I was feeling a little sheepish for not realizing what the crowd had been applauding. In fairness, it was my first time performing as a mascot before a crowd of this size and I was not yet used to the reactions my antics could elicit from so many people.

The crowd's response and my reaction to it helped drive home several of the lessons I had learned at camp, namely: your actions can have a real effect on a crowd; no matter how absurd or mistaken your actions may be (like looking for the team coming onto the field), just make it appear as if you intended to do it for comic effect; and no matter what, just keep going.

After recovering from my momentary confusion, I strode up and down the track thanking the band and high fiving many of its members as they made their way up into the stands. Then I grabbed my canvas bag and ran up into the stands tossing candy in every direction. I even ran up into the upper deck and tossed candy there as well. Several people later told me that they thought it might have been the first time any Quaker had gone into the upper deck.

After emptying my canvas bag, I raced back onto the field. By now, I was sweating and feeling a little bit nauseated from a combination of the warm, muggy weather and all the running around in such close proximity to my break-fast meal. I grabbed a cup of Gatorade and ice and sipped a little bit of it before seeing the football team come out into the runway about to enter the field from the locker room.

I dropped the cup and started running in the team's direction hoping desperately that I wouldn't toss my cookies. I was starting to feel something rise up in my throat as I arrived at the team's runway. "Oh no!" I thought. "If I lose it, that will be my legacy. Nothing I do for the rest of the year will cause people to forget if I heave on Opening Night."

Fortunately, I caught a break. The football players were waiting for their coaches to come out of the locker room. It gave me a chance to catch my breath and calm my nausea down a bit. The players around me were loosening their limbs and turning and nodding their heads.

The coaches exited the locker room. It was time to start running again. I ran out on the field just ahead of the team as the band played "Fight On, Pennsylvania." Reaching the sidelines, I was soaked in sweat. Back to the Gatorade, I drank and sucked on some ice cubes as the nausea finally subsided. "Whew!" I thought. "Disaster averted."

The game got underway, and I began Quaker-walking up and down the sideline behind the team, peeking over their shoulders and between them from time to time to see the game. About midway through the first quarter, Penn recovered a fumble by one the best running backs in the league, Cornell's Derrick Harmon (drafted by the San Francisco 49ers in 1984). Four plays later, Penn scored the first touchdown of the season. I yelled to the four male cheerleaders to follow me to the end zone in which Penn had just scored and Quaker-walked down to the goal line.

After placekicker Dave Shulman made the extra point, I began leaping in the air with arms raised in celebration of the score pretending to be oblivious to the four cheerleaders who almost immediately grabbed me, picked me off the ground, and ran with me hanging between them straight down the goal line toward the center of the field. As we neared the middle, they turned and ran through the end zone directly toward the goalpost. It was at this point that Claude had the band's rhythm section play a drum roll. And as the cheerleaders swung me, crotch first, into the goalpost, there was the cymbals crash I had asked for, perfectly timed according to plan. Much to my surprise, two other things occurred that I hadn't counted on. First, the impact with the goalpost was so hard that the goalpost visibly shook and, second, simultaneous with my hitting the goalpost the crowd collectively emitted a loud groan, "Ohhhh!!!!!"

I stayed motionless on the ground, flat on my back, for a moment as the cheerleaders scampered away. When the band broke into the song they traditionally play after Penn touchdowns, "Hang, Jeff," I popped back up and walked backed to the sideline, arms swinging, as the crowd cheered. The stunt was a success! We got to repeat it in the second quarter as Penn took a 14-0 lead. Once again, the crowd reacted with a loud groan and, once again, the crowd cheered when I popped up and returned to the sideline.

The goalpost ramming routine expertly performed by cheerleaders (l to r) David Furfine, Brad Bovee and Wayne Firsty (fourth cheerleader hidden by goalpost).
Photo courtesy of Poor Richard's Record

The rest of the half past uneventfully. During halftime, I joined the band on the field as my own one-man Quaker kazoo section. I think it was the first time a Quaker had seamlessly merged into the band for a halftime performance. The crowd AND the band loved it!

In the third quarter, the cheerleaders and I got to repeat the goalpost ramming routine when Penn scored its third touchdown of the game. When the third quarter ended, I greeted members of the freshman class as they made their way down from the stands and onto the track to participate in a Penn tradition - one with which they were not yet familiar. After the third quarter of every football game, Penn fans, led by the band, join in the singing of "Drink a Highball." According to Penn's Office of Student Affairs:

> In years long past, students would literally make a toast with the drink to the success of Penn's athletic teams. During Prohibition, stubborn students insisted on keeping their tradition – since they could not use alcohol, they had no choice but to literally "toast" Penn. As the last line, "Here's a toast to dear old Penn," is sung, the fans send toast hurling through the air onto the sidelines.

In a slight twist, when this tradition is performed during the first home game of the year, the unsuspecting freshman class is invited to march around the track and is then pummeled with toast by the upperclassman. In the last home game of the year, the freshmen are led to believe they will get their revenge, when the seniors are invited down onto the track. Much to the chagrin of the freshmen, however, the experienced seniors know better and open umbrellas just as the triggering line of the song is being sung. The hurled toast is deflected harmlessly away.

After all the toast was cleaned up and the fourth quarter of the game began, Penn scored one more touchdown and the crowd witnessed one more goalpost ramming. Penn won the game 28-7. It was a good start to the season for the Red and Blue and a good start for the new Quaker!

When the game ended, I was exhausted and decided not to stick around for the post-game fireworks show. Walking back home through campus still in my Quaker outfit (and, therefore, still in character and doing the Quaker-walk), people approached me with high-fives, "nice goings," and "how did you do that goalpost thing." I returned the high-fives, thanked people for the "nice goings" and refused to answer the questions about the goalpost routine. Once home, I went directly to my room, peeled off the sweat-soaked costume and took a long hot shower.

After my shower, I threw on a t-shirt and some shorts and went down to the kitchen. It was time for a nice, cold beer. Lowell was in the kitchen when I walked in.

"You were good," he said with a smile.

"Thanks," I replied while opening a Miller Lite (which was more like water than beer, but what did I know then).

"It was really cool when you broke through the paper on the side of the drum," he said.

"That wasn't paper. The drum is made of wood. I had a door cut in it and dropped it down when I popped out."

"Really?" Lowell asked incredulously. "I didn't see that. It just looked like you burst through. You really couldn't tell."

"That's great! I was really worried how it would look. The fact that you didn't see the door is awesome. That's what I was shooting for." I was elated.

"And how'd you do that thing with the goalposts without killing yourself?"

"Sorry. Trade secret."

"Heh, heh. Aw c'mon."

"Nope. Sorry. I'll only tell the next Quaker and, maybe, someday a son of mine if he gets into Penn so that he, too, could do the routine as the Quaker if he wants to."

We both laughed as I downed the rest of my beer and headed back upstairs. I collapsed into bed with game one under my belt and fell into what proved to be a good, deep sleep.

Of course, amid all the fun and frivolity on game days, I still needed to go to my classes and study. One morning following the Cornell game, I arrived a couple of minutes early to my Urban Economics class. The professor (whose name I confess I cannot remember) came over to where I was sitting as students continued to file into the classroom.

 "Thank you for giving candy to my grandson!" he exclaimed. "He was so excited! It was a big thrill for him!"

"I'm so glad!" I responded with a smile having had no idea who the professor's grandson was, nor was I aware of the fact that he had attended Saturday's game.

As the professor was returning to the front of the class, he stopped, turned around, and loudly asked me, "By the way, how do you do that goalpost trick without getting hurt?"

"Well, my transcript says that I am from West Hartford, but I'm really from Krypton!" I quipped.

"Very good, Mr. Becker!" my professor said. With a smile and a nod, he proceeded to start his lecture.

Chapter 9 – Mopping Up at Giants Stadium

The following week was Penn's first away game of the season. It was in Newark, Delaware – yes, Delaware not New Jersey. I called the University of Delaware's athletic department mid-week to explain the goalpost routine and to obtain permission to run onto the field to perform it. This was a habit I would follow for every away game. After getting over her initial incredulity at the stunt, The woman in the Delaware athletic department said, "No problem" and that she would let the university's security know what might be in store on Saturday. While I, in fact, had no trouble with Delaware's security, the football team had a load of trouble with the Blue Hens and got smoked 40-7. As a result, the cheerleaders and I only had one opportunity to perform the goalpost routine, but at least that went well.

Up next was a Saturday night away game against the Columbia Lions. Ordinarily, the game would have been played at Columbia's Baker Field in Harlem, but their home stadium was under renovation, so the game was moved to Giants Stadium in the New Jersey Meadowlands. This made for a shorter drive for us coming up the Jersey Turnpike from Philadelphia.

The cheerleading squad always traveled in an athletic department van. For insurance reasons, the school wanted someone who was at least 21 years old to drive. That pretty much left the driving up to the seniors, of which I was one.

Saturday October 1, 1983 was soggy. It wasn't much fun driving up the Jersey Turnpike in the pouring rain. We passed several accidents along the way. Thankfully, we arrived without being in one of them.

I wore shorts and a t-shirt riding up and put my Quaker costume on in the van before disembarking for the game. We entered the stadium through the team entrance. Walking out of the tunnel and into the brightly lit stadium I scanned the stands. The weather kept the crowd size down to just over 7000. Everyone there easily fit into the lower deck.

There being no easy way to climb into the stands from the field, I tossed candy to the crowd from below the ten-foot high wall separating us and leapt to high-five fans reaching low over the wall – each time landing with a splash on the soaked turf.

Through a steady rain, Penn took command in the first half of the game with three touchdown passes to a fellow Connecticut native, wide receiver Karl Hall. Karl was perhaps the fastest player on the field. On this night, he just couldn't be caught.

After each of the touchdowns, my male cheerleader cohorts and I performed the goalpost routine and I was soaked to the skin after being repeatedly dropped in puddles. About midway through the second quarter while contemplating what I should do to entertain the crowd, I remembered back to something I had learned at cheerleading camp and borrowed a white hand towel from one of the trainers. I noticed stadium security was standing and facing the crowd about every 20 yards or so midway between the field and the stands all along the sideline.

Each of the security team members wore a yellow slicker and each, of course, was wearing his hood.

I walked up behind one of the security guards with the towel in my hand and held it over his head. Then, without ever touching him, I began making slow circular motions with the towel just inches above him so that from the stands it looked as if I were shining his head. He had no idea what was going on as more and more people in the stands started looking, pointing, and laughing at him. After a minute or two, the flustered security guard turned and saw me. Busted!

I leapt back, then took a couple quick steps back toward the guard, smiled and shook his hand. He laughed and I turned and made my way back to the trainer to return the now drenched towel.

In the second half, the skies really opened up. It poured so hard that huge puddles developed along the sidelines. This gave me another idea.

I went back into the nearest tunnel and found a member of the Giants Stadium grounds crew and asked, "Do you have a mop I could borrow?"

"Sure," he replied and then disappeared into a utility closet down the hallway under the stands. A moment later he reappeared and handed me a long string mop. "Here!"

"Thanks, it's perfect," I said grabbing it and hurrying back onto the field. Mop in hand I walked over to the sidelines and began mopping the puddles occasionally asking a trainer or other football staffer to momentarily step aside so that I could mop in the area in which they had been standing. Occasionally, I'd sneak a peek at the stands and saw that people were really into it – pointing and laughing at what was going on.

As Penn finished off a 35-10 victory, the rain became a drizzle and then only a mist. It was at the end of the game that one of my personal most memorable moments of the year happened. Bounding down one of the aisles was a curly-haired man yelling out my name. It was Ricky Berman. He had been the Quaker my sophomore year and was the best that I had seen. He was hilarious.

"Ricky! It's great to see you! I had no idea you were here!" I said as he reached the wall.

"Brian," he said, "I just had to come down to tell you what a great job you're doing! I wish I had thought of half the things you did out there tonight. It was amazing!"

"Thanks, Ricky! I always thought you were the best, so it really means a lot to me coming from you. Thanks so much for coming down and telling me. I really appreciate it."

Ricky gave me a thumbs-up and, on that note, we went our separate ways. But Ricky's kind comments were a special gift that I have never forgotten.

Chapter 10 – Penthouse Magazine Sends "Apology" to Penn

On Mondays following football games, I would bring my costume into the equipment room in the Palestra and leave it with the staff person there to be cleaned. It was invariably soaked with sweat from all my running around. On the Monday following the Columbia game, I noticed the heavy rain had taken a toll on my hat. The side brims were no longer curled up. Rather they were droopy. All my attempts at re-curling them failed. As a last resort, I took a needle and some thread and stitched the brims to sides of the hat's crown to re-form the triangular appearance that was necessary. It wasn't perfect but it would do. The situation would eventually be rectified during basketball season in an unexpected way as you will find out a little later.

As the week wore on, word spread that we would have some special guests at the Brown game on Saturday. Larry Linderman, a writer, was coming to the school "to apologize" for an article he had written a year earlier entitled, "20 Worst College Football Teams." The article had appeared in the October 1982 issue of Penthouse Magazine, and Larry had picked Penn to be the third worst team in the country that year. Notoriously, Larry compared Penn's team to "a thoroughbred with four broken legs."

Contrary to Larry's prognostication, however, Penn football went on to its most successful season since 1959 and won a share of the Ivy League title. This led to Larry's apology trip to Penn. Word also had it that he wasn't coming alone. He was bringing along some attractive company – a couple of centerfolds a/k/a Penthouse "pets." When this information reached the Penn Band room some creative minds got to work.

The Penn Precision Marching Band, like every other "marching" band in the Ivy League, except Cornell's,[9] didn't actually march. Instead, when it performed its members would scatter around the field and arrive at his or her assigned spot only when the drums played a rhythm that was a sharp "Rat-a-tat-a-tat! Rat-a-tat-a-tat! Tat! Tat! Tat!" Each member would be in position by the end of the first "Tat" and would swing his or her right leg up to the right on the second "Tat" and return it to the ground on the third and final "Tat." This last part demonstrated the "precision" part of the band's name.

Each halftime, the band's show would have a theme usually centered on current events. An announcer would read a humorous script and the band's formation and/or musical number would deliver the punch line. Knowing that Penthouse

---

[9] Cornell's band wore formal band uniforms and militaristically marched around the field in rigid formations like most high school and college marching bands in the country. The rest of the Ivy League's bands were far less formal. Their uniforms consisted of pants and sweaters or jackets that sometimes only loosely resembled uniforms, and they walked or ran around the field in a scattered fashion and generally demonstrated their disdain for standard marching band actions and procedures. As a result, Cornell's band was the outcast of the Ivy League. But apparently band counted as a gym requirement at Cornell. That explains a lot!

"pets" were going to be in attendance, the band's leaders designed their halftime show accordingly.

Game day was a sunny, pleasant October day. When I arrived, in costume, at the Annenberg Center courtyard, the drum major pulled me aside to tell me about the band's halftime plans. "We've got a special number planned for our guests," he said. "Would you mind escorting our female guests onto the field following our second number?"

"No problem," I replied with a smile. "Happy to help!"

After the traditional march through campus and our arrival at Franklin Field, after the pre-game festivities, including my tossing candy to the crowd, and after fans were settling in for the game, all eyes were on the lookout for the special guests. Part way through the first quarter, they came into the stadium and quietly made their way to the stands taking seats just a couple of rows off the field. The writer, Larry, was a middle-aged non-descript white man who wore slacks and a shirt. The ladies accompanying him were gorgeous twenty-somethings who wore knee-length dresses – the tall lithe blonde wore a pink one and the shorter, brown-haired beauty a blue one. The blue-eyed blonde was Linda Kenton, and the brunette was Sheila Kennedy. Both had been Penthouse centerfolds and over the next couple of years each would be named "Penthouse Pet of the Year" – a high honor in that field.

At halftime of the hard-fought game, which would eventually end in a 24-24 tie (and three more goalpost rammings), I made my way over to our female guests. As I approached them, I slowed my walk, but did not stop. Walking by, I gave them an exaggerated wink bringing smiles to their faces and chuckles from the crowd. I returned to them, again, as the band made its way onto the field and this time stopped, introduced myself and told them that I had been asked by the band to bring them down onto the field to be recognized as part of the band's halftime show. Initially they balked, but after a little coaxing and reassurance from me that I would stay with them and guide them along, each woman took one of my arms and I escorted them down to the track with my chest pumped out and a grin across my face.

At this point photographers from the school paper, the Daily Pennsylvanian a/k/a the DP, and from the yearbook, Poor Richard's Record, were snapping photos of us.[10] I put my arms around each of the women and smiled for the cameras. Then we stood together awaiting the signal from the drum major to join the band on the field.

After the band finished playing its second song, the signal came, and I walked the lovely ladies onto the field where we stood in front of the band and turned to face the home crowd just as the announcer was finishing reading the script explaining the appearance of the two women with me. With that the band began playing the J. Geil's Band hit, "Centerfold." The two live centerfolds beside me began to giggle and then, being the good sports they were, danced with me on the field throughout the song. Man, was I one lucky guy – and all in the name of just doing my job!

When the song concluded, each of the women grabbed one of my arms again and back to the stands we went. I didn't want this experience to end. And so, on our walk back, I thought, "What the heck?" I stopped, and with adrenaline pumping,

---

[10] Unfortunately, I've been unable to locate any of the photos taken or I would have shared them with you here.

heart racing, and all the chutzpah I could muster, I said, "If you ladies will still be around this evening, you're invited to a party at my house off campus. We're expecting a big crowd and it should be fun."

For a moment it appeared they were considering it, but then Sheila let me down very nicely stating, "We'd love to, but we're going to be leaving right after the game."

"Too bad," I replied. "Everyone wants to know about Blimpy[11] the mechanical sheep" (which was our announced theme in flyers put up around campus) "and I'd introduce you to him. Oh well!" After they each gave me an incredulous look, we continued our way up into the stands and they returned to their seats. Mission accomplished!

---

[11] The idea for the bizarre theme was the brainchild of one of my housemates, Walt, who managed to convince the rest of us that something as weird as "Blimpy the mechanical sheep" would create a buzz, pique people's interest, and draw a large crowd to our house for the party. Strange as it may seem, Walt was right! Our place was packed that night and we ended up running out of beer and refreshments shortly after midnight.

Chapter 11 – A Homecoming (of sorts) at Yale

I had circled Saturday, October 22nd on my calendar. We were playing Yale at the Yale Bowl in New Haven, Connecticut. The Yale Bowl was only about 45 minutes away from my parents' home in West Hartford and I hoped they would make it to the game.

I grew up in a lower middle-class family. Neither of my parents, though both very bright, had gone to college. My mom graduated from high school and went on to become a licensed beautician. My dad didn't even graduate from high school.

I was told my paternal grandfather[12] had a series of health issues that prevented him from working a steady job from the time my dad was 10. As a result, dad picked up different jobs throughout his school years to help his mom put food on the table for the family of four. Dad also was an athlete. He played football and baseball at Hall High School.[13] He also liked girls. According

---

[12] I never met either of my grandfathers, both of whom died at age 59 the summer before I was born, exactly two weeks apart and only months after my parents married at the ripe old ages of 21 and 19.

[13] He was good enough to get a tryout with the Red Sox after high school but rejected an opportunity to play in the minors since he wanted to get a "real job" so that he could marry my mother.

to my mother, this combination wreaked havoc with my dad's studies and prevented him from graduating. Looking back and knowing what I know now, I wouldn't be surprised if my dad also suffered from ADHD of the inattentive variety and that, too, played a role in his failure to graduate from high school.[14] While dad didn't graduate, he eventually earned a GED.

Dad's work career was a series of ups and downs. He had several different jobs, mostly in sales. There were times when he was without a steady job and during some of those times my family struggled to make ends meet. But we never went hungry. And that was due to my superhero – my mom. My mom is a wonderful person. She is one of the most positive people you could ever meet. This is even more amazing because she experienced several potentially devastating traumas throughout her life.

Mom was born into a lower middle-class family, too. Her dad was an immigrant from Kyiv and her mom was a first generation American. Mom spent the better part of the first year of her life in an orphanage because her mother was too ill to care for her, and her father had his hands full raising her nearly one-year older sister, my Auntie Fay. As a kid, mom was a fierce competitor, entering and winning running races to win flour for her mother.

When mom was only 11 years old, her mom died suddenly of a cerebral hemorrhage. Despite that, she carried a cheery

---

[14] Whether my dad suffered from attention deficit hyperactive disorder ("ADHD") is something we will never know as he died unexpectedly in 1997 (two days before his 58th birthday), which was long before I was aware of the extent ADHD could affect a person's ability to focus on things like schoolwork.

disposition into high school and was a leader on the Weaver High School cheerleading squad (which is where my dad first saw her at a basketball game between Weaver and Hall). She had thoughts of becoming a nurse but given her family's financial circumstances when she graduated from high school, she opted for cosmetology school instead.

As I mentioned earlier, my mom was only 19 when she married my dad in 1961. They got pregnant on their honeymoon. Then, less than three months later, on July 6th, the day before my mom's twentieth birthday, her dad, whom she adored, died – also of a cerebral hemorrhage. The shock of that loss still hadn't worn off when my dad's father died two weeks later of uremic poisoning.

I was born in December of that year. And while I learned of these early tragedies as I got older, my parents never dwelt on them. Instead, my parents did their best to see the humor in situations and always emphasized the importance of an education.

From the time I can remember, my mom always read to me, helped teach me to read (as did my Auntie Fay), and encouraged me all along the way. She also taught me how to cook and do laundry. Knowing to separate the whites from the colors sure came in handy when girls in college couldn't understand why all their underwear had turned pink.

My dad taught me math through the speedometer in the car. He also planted the seed in my head to become a lawyer because, in his words, "it's a great background for any career and many of the top executives at major corporations have law degrees." He encouraged me to study hard and get good grades so that I might eventually go to college. And if I got into an Ivy League college, well, that would be about as good as it could get.

But as I mentioned earlier, my mom is my superhero because when times were tough, she was the one who held everything together. She earned the steady income as a hairdresser and eventually became a salon owner (which she remained for over 38 years). She always made sure there was food on the table. She also volunteered to help and comfort others on a regular basis – whether it was going to a terminally ill customer's home or hospital bed to "give them a lift" by styling their hair, cuddling premature babies, or being a hospice volunteer – all while maintaining her irrepressible positive attitude. She continued doing these good works even after my dad died and after she, herself, suffered serious health issues.

Mom also taught me never to give up no matter what life throws your way, to give it your best shot, and to keep a positive attitude. And mom doesn't just say those things. She lives them. I've always figured that if she could remain so upbeat and indefatigable after all she has been through,[15] then I should be able to do it, too.

All this information is just a very long prologue to the fact that my parents didn't have much money and they both worked long weeks - including Saturdays.   At the time, dad was a car salesman whose busiest day each week was Saturday. Saturday was mom's busiest day, too, as all the women wanted their hair done before going out on Saturday night or to church on Sunday

---

[15] Mom got remarried to a wonderful guy, Barry, in 2009. Unfortunately, Barry also died, but they had 10+ years of great times and companionship before that happened.

morning. As a result, neither one of them was able to come see me perform before my home crowd in Philadelphia.

While they would both have to miss work to see me at Yale, at least they wouldn't have to incur the expense of traveling to Philly and paying for an overnight hotel stay. I had given them the date of the Yale game before I left for school at summer's end, and asked if they could please try to come. They promised to try.

So, when I called on the Sunday before the Yale game, [16] I was thrilled to learn that each of my parents had arranged to miss work the following Saturday and would, in fact, be coming to the game with my sister, Dina! The morning of the Yale game, I met my family in the field that served as the parking lot to the Yale Bowl. As I walked over to them in full Quaker regalia, they smiled. My 17-year-old sister, decked out in red and blue clothing and hair ribbons ready to cheer on the Penn team, came bounding over. Hugs and kisses were exchanged all around.

Mom said, "You look good!" while nodding approvingly. My dad chuckled as he stepped back and looked at me from head to toe and back again. A moment later, as the Penn Band struck

---

[16] Throughout my collegiate career, I called my parents at my grandmother's place every week during their Sunday brunch. Nanny Sue, as I called her, would answer the phone, say, "Hello, goodbye!" and pass the phone off to my step-grandfather - often before I could even say anything to her because the long-distance call "costs too much money." Papa Bob, who married my grandmother when I was about three years old and was every bit a true grandfather to me, would always finish our almost equally brief conversation with "Keep up the good work!" and pass the phone to one of my parents, with whom I would have a lengthier conversation before speaking with my other parent and sister.

up the pep tune "Cheer, Pennsylvania!" before a group of alumni tailgating in the field, I said, "I'll see you inside," and high-tailed it over to join the rest of the cheerleading squad performing with the band.

Entering the Yale Bowl a short while later, I saw my family sitting about ten rows up on the Penn side of the field. It gave me an extra jolt of adrenaline to see them in the stands.

The game itself was a low scoring affair. About midway through the first quarter, Penn ran the ball into the end zone from the Yale two-yard line for the first score of the game. Following the extra point, I was jumping up and down near the goal line when the four male cheerleaders grabbed me to run the goalpost routine. After being smashed into the goalposts and being left for dead, I waited until the goalposts stopped swaying and then sprang back into action. Heading for the sidelines, I saw the Yale security guards laughing. It was the first time any of them had seen the routine. And the same was true for my family who pointed, laughed, and clapped with hands over their heads.

At halftime, Penn led 7-0. Rather than play kazoo on the field with the band, this time I went into the stands and climbed the steps to spend time with my family. They were all smiles when I arrived.

Then mom asked with a look of concern, "It doesn't hurt you when they do that, does it?"

"No, mom. I'm fine." I said while giving her another hug. "You'll still be able to have grandchildren."

"That was one of the funniest things I have ever seen!" exclaimed my father wiping tears from his eyes.

"Glad you liked it!" I gushed with a smile from ear to ear. "Hope I get to do it some more before the game is over."

As it turned out, I only got to do it one more time, but it didn't really matter, as Yale never scored. The final score was Penn 17, Yale 0.

My family came down to the field after the game. We had only a few minutes before I had to join the other cheerleaders at the squad's van to head back to Philly.

"Thanks for coming," I said. "I'm so glad you got a chance to see me perform!"

"It was great!" my father replied.

"So much fun and so proud of you," mom added.

"It was a goof! MY big brother," Dina said with a wide smile.

We hugged, kissed, and said our goodbyes. I headed back to the van happy that my family had come and had a good time.

My father's reaction to my Quaker performance reminded me of the time I was a junior in high school and played saxophone in the Hall High School Jazz Band. Each March, the band, together with a jazz choir and jazz dance troupe, puts on a show called Pops 'n Jazz. I came home from school one day in February and announced that tickets were going on sale for that year's show. When I asked which night my parents would like to come to the show, my father, unaware of band's reputation and the quality of the performance, laughed at the thought and responded, "Oompah, pah, oompah pah!" I'm sure he was still thinking of my days playing in a poorly tuned elementary school band. Little did he know what was in store. The Hall Concert Jazz Band couldn't have been any more different from the early elementary school experience. A number of its alumni have gone on to play professionally.[17]

Fast-forward to the scene a couple of weeks later. I walked into the house after the show he and my mom attended. Dad was waiting in the front hall and blurted out, "When can we get tickets for next year?!" I smiled and my chest swelled with pride.

---

[17] Hall High, to this day, is home to one of the nation's top high school music programs. From its inception in 1958, the Hall High School Concert Jazz Band has been, and remains, an internationally acclaimed group boasting numerous awards, winning many competitions (including those at Berklee College of Music and Lincoln Center). In 1978 (the year before I got into the band), Hall was named the top high school big band in the country by Downbeat Magazine and finished second in 1980 (my senior year). Each year, the band recorded an album at RCA Studio in New York until it built its own recording studio at the school in the late 1980s. It has toured Europe many times (including an 18-day concert tour during my senior year), performing in large auditoriums, in high school gymnasiums, in churches, on town greens, in U.S. military officers' clubs, and live on the BBC and Armed Forces Radio. Playing in that band for two years, mostly as the baritone sax player, was one of life's great experiences. Being the Quaker was another.

Chapter 12 – The Rest of a Championship Season: The Real Homecoming, the Prude Intrudes, Harvard Antics and a Regional Television Finale

Next up was Princeton on homecoming weekend. Before the game even began, there was added excitement for me. Earlier in the week, Stefan Fatsis, a sports reporter for the Daily Pennsylvanian, had come over to interview me. [18] The interview resulted in a large spread complete with several pictures in the Homecoming Edition of the paper that was out on newsstands all around campus early in the morning on game day. Unbeknownst to me some of my housemates had been interviewed, too, and had some nice and funny things to say. It was a good piece, and I was honored to be featured.[19]

---

[18] Stefan went on to become a professional journalist working for both the AP and the Wall Street Journal in addition to being a regular guest on National Public Radio's All Things Considered. He also has written three books and is an accomplished Scrabble player.

[19] I picked up some extra copies and sent one home to my parents and another to my best friend from high school, Andy. Andy's family owned a printing business. His dad, Bob, was nice enough to make a large copy of the article, which my parents had laminated and framed. It became an instant keepsake. A few years ago, the frame started falling apart so my wife and I got it reframed. That's the framed article you see me posing with beneath my Quaker costume in the last chapter of this book. You can still read the article online in the Daily Pennsylvanian's archives at:

Later at Franklin Field, the stands on the Penn side, upper and lower decks, were packed with over 38,000 fans. I felt my pulse racing as I Quakered before the raucous crowd – throwing out candy, doing the Quaker-walk, hooting and hollering, and getting rammed into the goalposts with each Quaker score.

The excitement built as the game remained close throughout. It was not decided until there were just 31 seconds left, when Princeton's two-point conversion attempt to win was squashed. On this key play, the Princeton quarterback took the snap, rolled to his right, and while looking for a receiver downfield, was sacked by a trio of Quakers led by our senior class president and

starting defensive tackle Dave "Bubba" Smith. The crowd, and yours truly, went wild – jumping, screaming, dancing, and screaming some more![20] The win enabled Penn to remain one game up on Harvard in the Ivy League standings with a showdown between the top two teams coming in two weeks.

Following the Homecoming game, while the exciting buzz was still reverberating through campus, I received an unexpected call from Ms. Dunflap the athletic department administrator who had been one of the judge's during tryouts and was nominally charged with oversight of the cheerleading squad. Ms. Dunflap was a modestly attractive blonde in her 30's. However, she carried herself in a rigid, pompous way that made her appear much older. As soon as she identified herself on the phone, I braced myself. No good ever comes from a Ms. Dunflap call.

"Brian?"

"Yes."

"This is Ms. Dunflap."

"Hello."

---

[20] You can see and hear some of the action from this moment by going to http://www.letsgoquakers.com/football1980s.htm and then scrolling down until you find the entry below. Once there, simply click on the video camera in the second to last column and enjoy!

| 0/29/1983 | PRINCETON | W 28-27 | COLOR FILM/WXPN RADIO AUDIO | SANDY FRIEDMAN JON HOCK | DVD | | 1:06:00 |

"I am calling to tell you that I don't want you getting rammed into the goalpost anymore. It's lewd, and we have children at the games!" she practically yelled at me.

"What?! You've gotta be kidding me!" I shot back. "It's the thing people have commented about most to me all season long. Everyone seems to enjoy it – even my professors (some of whom even bring their grandchildren to the games). I really want to keep doing it," I pleaded.

"Well, I'm not a fan of that," she replied.

"I understand Ms. Dunflap, but everyone else appears to be." I responded while trying to control an urge to scream. Running through my head were the names of people I would enlist to help me overturn Ms. Dunflap's position when, suddenly, she proposed an alternative.

"All right," she started, "I'll allow you to do it, but only once each half."

"What?!" I repeated. "How can you do that?! It'll be very strange if we score more than once each half and I only do it the first time." I was trying to win her over with my logic and an obvious hypothetical situation, but she wasn't biting.

"That's as far as I'm willing to go. If you don't like it, you can just stop doing it altogether," she replied.

"Fine," I said knowing full well that she would likely shoot me down completely if I continued to protest.

Hanging up the phone, I immediately called Steve, the cheerleading co-captain, to inform him of Ms. Dunflap's call.

"Noooooo," Steve reacted. "That sucks! But don't worry, Brian, we'll make it work."

Colgate rolled into town the following weekend. In an ugly game, Penn lost 34-20. As it turned out, Penn only scored one time more than my allotted goalpost rammings, so it wasn't so bad. But plenty of people noticed and asked me afterward why I wasn't rammed a third time. Needless to say, I was unhappy with the prude-imposed restriction. Having to be abide by this restriction was one of the few disappointments I faced as the Quaker.

Of course, being the Quaker did have some side benefits. In addition to getting invited to a lot of parties, most of which I politely declined to attend, I got a chance to interact with some beautiful women. When wearing the costume, I could go up to practically any woman and flirt – even if her boyfriend was standing or sitting right next to her. Many welcomed the attention. Here's a photo from my yearbook (Poor Richard's Record) standing with a lovely feature baton twirler, Amy Lewis, on the track at Franklin Field:

One of the perks of being the mascot.
Photo courtesy of Poor Richard's Record

There also were times where I could use my notoriety to get into
The Daily Pennsylvanian. The first was a letter to the editor to
correct a misrepresentation of the school's alma mater by the
paper's editor-in-chief. With tongue planted firmly in cheek,
here is what I wrote as it actually appeared in the paper on
November 9, 1983:

Where Are You, Pete?

To the Editor:

Where is the real Peter Canellos? Was he kidnapped
and disposed of in the same manner as Jimmy Hoffa, or is
he just enjoying a vacation somewhere in Greece?
Wherever he may be, he is definitely not here at Penn. The
man currently running *The Daily Pennsylvanian* must be a
cleverly disguised impostor because, after four years at
Penn, surely the *real* Peter Canellos would know that
"Hail! Pennsylvania!" (not "The Red and Blue," as stated
in the Mask and Wig article, November 4) is Penn's alma
mater. Where are you, Pete?

BRIAN BECKER
The Quaker
College '84

The following weekend was the showdown with Harvard. If
Penn won, it would clinch at least a tie for the Ivy title and Penn
could win the title outright with a victory over Dartmouth in the
final week.

November 12, 1983 in Cambridge, Massachusetts was a gray,
raw day. The temperature at game time was in the low 40's and
dropped into the 30s during the game. That might have been
tolerable if it weren't for the wind blowing out of the northwest
at 25-30 mph, gusting to around 40 mph. The wind chill made
it feel, at times, like it was in the single digits.

Wearing thermal underwear under my Quaker costume and
moving around the field and the stands with my rapid Quaker-

walk provided little relief. I still froze. Making things worse, as the afternoon wore on, there was little to cheer about. Penn was getting manhandled on the field and wound up losing 28-0. Once again, the Dunflap-imposed goal post ramming limit failed to come into play.

It felt almost as bad as the 45-7 drubbing Penn had taken two years earlier during my first trip up to Harvard with the Penn Band. The most memorable part of that weekend had nothing to do with football. It was the ride up and the wait for our hosts outside the Harvard band room that I will always remember.

The Penn Band travelled to away games in two coach buses. One was the "study" bus, which was intended for those who wished to read, sleep, daydream or engage in quiet conversation. The other was the "party" bus, affectionately referred to as the PGA bus, home to the Penn Gangbang Association (political correctness had not yet been discovered), which transported the rowdier members of the band.

The PGA bus was one huge party that ran from the time the bus pulled out of West Philly until it came to a stop at the ultimate destination. Each party had a different theme. The theme for the mid-November Harvard trip, which would last approximately 7 hours, was "Malibu Beach Party."

After loading our musical instruments and overnight bags into the storage compartments under the passenger section, we started hauling our supplies for the party on to the bus: snacks, cups, napkins, leis, a full keg, and a bag of sand to be dumped onto the floor – the latter item, the bus driver blocked from reaching its destination. With everything aboard the bus and about 50 hearty souls ready to go, the bus pulled onto the road.

Band members immediately removed their outer clothing revealing bathing suits and t-shirts. Leis were donned, cups were passed out and people made their way to the back of the bus where the beer was already flowing. Eating, drinking, and singing songs from the PGA's obscene songbook were a great way to pass the time. As the bus slowed down at every toll booth (and there were many – particularly on the NJ Turnpike), the whole bus would chant in one loud singsong voice, "TOLL BOOTH! TOLL BOOTH!" and then erupt into the toll booth song whose lyrics – written by our best and brightest - went something like this, "Goooooooooooooooood morning! Good morning! How'd you like to bite my ass?! Good morning, good morning! How'd you like to bite my ass?! One, two, f#*k you! Three, four on the floor! Five, six, OOOOOHHH go f#*k yourself!" Then we'd look out the windows to see the toll collector's expression. It usually was a head shaking smirk.

The last stop on the Jersey Turnpike before heading into New York was home to the Vince Lombardi Rest Stop. This rest stop is much like every other one on the turnpike. It was a single story, flat-roofed, brick and glass building next to several rows of gas pumps and a large parking lot. But this stop was different in a very big way. In its lobby was a trophy case that housed Vince Lombardi memorabilia.

After two and half hours of non-stop eating and drinking, it was the perfect place to empty one's bladder. It also enabled us to carry on another longtime Penn Band tradition, which occurred on each football away trip north of Princeton. After all the band members had a chance to take care of their business at the rest stop, we would gather around the trophy case to try to channel the legendary Hall of Fame coach by chanting "Vince! Vince! Vince! Vince! Vince! Vince! Vince! Vince!"

The drum major would then yell, "Vince, help our offense!"

To which the band would scream, "Offense!"

Drum major: "Vince, help our defense!"

Band: "Defense!"

And then the "Vince!" chanting would resume. This would continue on and on, while other rest stop patrons would gawk at the strange scene until the rest stop's manager would invariably come and throw us out for making too much noise and impeding the flow of patrons.

After getting the heave ho, we quickly headed back onto the bus and resumed drinking, eating, singing, and drinking some more all the way up to Cambridge. At the conclusion of each bus ride, the PGA was always sure to thank our bus driver on our way off the bus with "The Bus Driver Song." It was sung to the tune of the folk song, "Did You Ever See a Lassie" and went like this:

Hooray for the bus driver, the bus driver, the bus driver!
Hooray for the bus driver, we hope he gets laid!
He works hard.
He plays hard.
He never can stay hard!
Hooray for the bus driver we hope he gets laid!

Hooray for the bus driver, the bus driver, the bus driver!
Hooray for the bus driver, we hope he gets laid!
He's happy.
He's jolly.
He's horny, by golly!

Hooray for the bus driver we hope he gets laid!

Our bus drivers were usually good sports and would smile and nod to us as we departed the bus. Not sure whether that was actual appreciation for the sentiments in the song or just relief that he was finally rid of us.

By the time we arrived at Harvard Yard, night had fallen. We disembarked onto the sidewalk outside the Harvard band room. When Ivy bands travel, members generally stay with counterparts from the host school's band. On this night, no one from the Harvard band was waiting for us. Calls were made to our contacts at Harvard to let them know we were there.

Big mistake making us wait. Leaving a bunch of happily drunk, creative college students with nothing to do for more than a couple of minutes was just asking for trouble. Just after our bus pulled away, we noticed that the street we were on was one-way and lined with parked cars – one of which was a VW bug.

About a dozen of us thought it would be fun to turn the bug around. So, we grabbed the car by the bumpers, picked it up, turned it around and left it backwards in the parking space. No sooner had we finished when a squad car carrying Cambridge's finest came down the street. One of the police officers glanced over at us and noticed the car parked backwards. Because there was another car behind the squad car, the cops didn't stop.

As soon as the police were out of sight, several of us felt a little remorse about our misdeed. We didn't want the unknown owner getting a ticket for parking the wrong way on a one-way street when he or she hadn't, in reality, parked the wrong way. So, we hurried over and turned the car back around.

No sooner had we finished when, once again, the squad car came down the street. It must have just gone around the block. Upon pulling alongside the VW, the officer who had originally seen the car parked backwards did a double take as he now saw it parked in the proper direction. At just that moment, our hosts arrived, and we laughed all the way into the Harvard band room where we were matched up with our hosts for the night. And we never got caught for our little auto antics.

Following the loss at Harvard, Penn still had one more game. The last week of the season had us at home against Dartmouth. A win would ensure at least a share of the Ivy League Championship. The game was being broadcast regionally on network TV by ABC Sports.[21]

With a chance at the Ivy title, the crowd that day was nearly as large as the one we had on Homecoming. Also, it being the last game for all the seniors, a pre-game ceremony was held during which the public address announcer called out the name and number of each senior on the team. As each name was called the player came forward, met his parents on the track and walked arm-in-arm with them to meet Sheldon Hackney, the University President, who shook hands with each player and

---

[21] You can see and hear a short snippet from this game (including seeing the cheerleaders running away after ramming me into the goalpost just before the ABC Sports logo and score appear on the screen toward the end of clip) by going to http://www.letsgoquakers.com/football1980s.htm, scrolling down until you find the entry below and clicking on the video camera in the second to last column.

11/19/1983	DARTMOUTH	W 38-14	QUAKERS WIN A SHARE OF IVY LEAGUE TITLE	ABC	STEVE GRAD DON TOLLEFSON	DL		2:34:41

each parent and presented each mother with a bouquet of flowers.

I stood a few feet beyond Hackney and congratulated each group of player/parents, too, essentially mimicking the University President. Much to my shock and delight, nearly every single parent – including the MOTHERS – said "We hope you get your balls crushed today!" The clear wish being that Penn would score a lot of points and win big.

After the pre-game ceremony, I beelined over to the male cheerleaders and relayed what the parents had said to me. "I don't care what Ms. Dunflap said, I want you to ram me into the goalposts after EVERY score today," I told them. "I'll take any flak the Athletic Department wants to throw at us. After all, I'm a senior and this is my last football game. What are they going to do to me?"

"Are you sure?" a couple of cheerleaders asked me. I nodded and smiled with two thumbs up. We were on!!

And, boy, were we. Penn rolled to a 38-14 victory and a share of the Ivy League Championship. Getting rammed repeatedly into the goalposts never felt so good. It was a great day! We had a great time, and no one ever said "boo" about the excessive goalpost rammings that took place!

Following the championship excitement, it was back to the grindstone. With mid-term exams approaching, I headed for the Van Pelt Library to start studying. Walking along the bustling path through college green it seemed as though I was exchanging hellos or head nods with every other person I passed. This was a dream come true and a far cry from the first day of my freshman year when I walked the same path knowing no one. Seeing upperclassmen greeting one another en route to and from classes, I was envious of them and had made a mental note that someday I'd like to be in a similar position. Thinking about that now, I smiled.

I entered the library and made my way through the turnstiles and up to the third floor. After settling in to work at an out-of-the-way table, I looked up from my book to see a student who I did not know looking at me. I resumed reading, but when I looked up again a moment later, the same guy was standing right across the table just staring at me.

"It's, …, it's the Quaker!!!" he shouted while pointing at me.

Quickly looking over my right shoulder, I yelled, "Where?"

Turning back to the unknown student, I caught a momentary look of puzzled astonishment after which he asked, "You ARE the Quaker, right?"

"Yes," I admitted. "But I've got to study now."

With a broad smile on his face, the student nodded his head. "O.k., thanks," he said. He complied with my request and walked away with a slight skip to his step.

At that point, I decided I should probably finish studying at home, packed up my stuff and left the library. It's fun getting noticed, but sometimes you really need to focus on what you are doing. This was one of those times.

Chapter 13 – Doing Some Good

Being the Quaker was a unique experience. Out of approximately 8000 undergraduates and 12,000 graduate students at the university in 1983-1984, I was the only person who, by virtue of donning a costume, instantly represented the entire school. This gave me opportunities to do things I otherwise would never have been able to do.

In Judaism, there is a concept known as "tikkun olam," which means "repair the world." It means we should be G-d's partners in helping to perfect the world by reaching out to those in need, righting wrongs and making a positive difference, no matter how small, in our community. In other words, go out and do good.

Over the course of the year, in addition to having fun, leading cheers, and performing at athletic events, I tried to do some good in Philadelphia. After football season, I decided to call the mascots from the other Big Five schools[22] and invite them over to the Children's Hospital of Philadelphia (CHOP) to spend some time visiting with patients. I started by calling CHOP.

---

[22] The Big Five was composed of Philadelphia universities Penn, LaSalle, St. Joseph's, Temple, and Villanova and, collectively, they had an intense intercity rivalry in basketball. The basketball teams played each other once every year with city bragging rights on the line.

"Hello. How may I direct your call?" a voice on the other end of the phone asked.

"Well, I'm not quite sure," I responded and proceeded to explain my proposal.

"I'll put you through to the hospital administrator's office," came the reply.

"Thank you."

"Hospital administrator's office, Julia speaking."

"Hi, Julia. My name is Brian Becker, and I am the Penn Quaker – the school's mascot," I began. "I'm calling to find out if the hospital would be amenable to the Big Five mascots – or as many of them as I can get – coming to visit the kids at the hospital. Would that be something the hospital would be interested in?"

"Would you please hold for a moment?" Julia asked.

"Sure, no problem."

A couple of minutes later, Julia got back on the line, "We would be delighted if you would come visit the kids. They'll be so excited."

"That's great!" I replied. "But please remember I don't have anyone else's commitment yet. I first wanted to be sure it was o.k. with CHOP."

"We understand. When would you want to come?"

"How 'bout next Thursday afternoon – around 3 o'clock?" I asked.

"That'll work."

"Great! I'll give you a call to confirm after I call the other mascots and I'll let you know. O.k.?"

"That'll be terrific. I'll wait to hear from you," Julia said.

"Thank you for your help," I said as I hung up the phone. I was excited to get the hospital's permission so easily. Now I had to get ahold of the other mascots.

Earlier in the year I received a call from Ms. Dunflap passing along an invitation the Penn Athletic Department had received asking if I would like to appear at the Grand Opening of the new King of Prussia mall. I thought she was joking, but after understanding she was serious, I turned down the invitation making it clear that I did not think it was appropriate for me, as a representative of Penn, to appear at an event for the benefit of a commercial enterprise. I told her I was only interested in going to charitable events.

Remembering this experience, I figured the best way to reach the other mascots was to go through the other schools' athletic departments. After a few hours of phone calls, leaving messages, and speaking with each mascot, I finally had everyone on board. I called and let Julia know we would be coming. And so, on that following Thursday afternoon, five nondescript college students walked into CHOP with duffel bags. In addition to my duffel bag, I also brought along a bunch of balloons.

We met in a small room on the main floor, introduced ourselves and changed into the LaSalle Explorer (who looked much like a commodore), the St. Joseph's Hawk (who kept his wings flapping once in costume), the Temple Owl (a real hoot), the Villanova Wildcat (whose head bore a ferocious looking face) and, of course, the Penn Quaker. Once we were in our costumes, and I grabbed the bunch of the balloons I had brought, a nurse escorted us out of our changing room and down the brightly lit hallway to visit patients in their rooms.

The first kid we met was a little boy sitting in a chair with his arm hooked up to bag of clear fluid hanging from a stand on wheels. He was probably seven or eight years old, with dark hair and darker eyes. On the whiteboard above his head was written "Patient's Name: Rocky."

"Hi, Rocky!" I said in a bright tone as we all piled into his room. "How ya doin' today?"

"Wow!" Rocky exclaimed. He stood up smiling from ear to ear as I handed him a balloon.

Each of us shook hands with him and moved about the room in our mascot modes. As we started to head for the door to go see the next patient, Rocky asked his nurse, "Can I go with them?"

"Sure," she replied.

The mascot group now had its own hospital mascot – Rocky! He followed us from room to room, up and down the hallway, holding on to the metal pole of his IV bag stand as we visited each of the other patients. Rocky was one of the luckier kids on the floor, as he seemed to be doing relatively well at the moment and had a lot of energy to follow us around.

Some kids were stuck in their chairs. Some were bedridden. As we left a room, I handed each child a balloon. When we entered one of the rooms, a small, thin boy propped up on the pillows in his bed screamed in horror and began crying when he saw the Wildcat. I pretended to be scared, too, crouching near the boy. Shielding both of us with my hands, I shooed the Wildcat out of the room. The boy calmed down after a couple of minutes. Because I felt badly that the visit frightened him, I left him with <u>two</u> balloons.

I was trailing the group as the mascot posse made its way down the hallway, when I heard a door open behind me. A nurse came out the door and raced toward me.

"Would you please come back and stand by that window?" she asked pointing to a large window next to the door she had emerged from. "I have a patient in there, Freddy, who's in isolation. He saw you walking by and asked if he could see you."

"Sure," I replied and called to the other mascots and explained the situation to them as the nurse went back into Freddy's room.

We crowded around the window and waved to Freddy. He stared at us and waved back. He was hooked up to some scary looking machines and wore an oxygen mask.

After a couple of minutes, the nurse came out of the room again. "Thank you so much. It means a lot to him. He sees you on tv all the time and is a big fan."

"Can he have a balloon?" I asked.

"No, we can't bring anything into the room that is not sterilized. Sorry, "she replied.

"O.k. but let him know we would have given him one if we could."

"I will," said the nurse. "Thanks, again."

"No, thank YOU for getting us to come over here. And please tell Freddy we hope he feels better soon," I said as we waved goodbye to Freddy and moved down the hallway.

We continued going room to room for a couple of hours. Seeing all the sick kids made the time feel more like a couple of days. Some were in better condition than others, but all were seriously ill. My heart felt heavy even as we tried to keep the mood light. I masked my pain with a smile and a balloon for each child we met.

At the end of our tour, we bid goodbye to Rocky, and a nurse thanked us for coming. She said it was a great distraction for the kids. After we returned to our room and changed into our street clothes, I thanked the other mascots for participating, and we went our separate ways.

When I got back to my off-campus house, I went up to my room and curled up in a ball on my bed. Seeing all those really sick kids affected me so much that I literally felt physically ill for the next few days. My housemates tried consoling me to no avail. As much as I knew that the other mascots and I had done a good thing going to visit the kids, I just couldn't bring myself to do it again. Upon further reflection, I wish I had been better able to emotionally handle the hospital visit so that I could have organized another visit or two later in the year.

Fortunately, I had other opportunities to help kids in different circumstances. For example, I participated in a bowling tournament for disabled children sponsored by McDonald's at a nearby bowling alley. Bowling in costume, I helped some children who had difficulty handling the ball by themselves bowl, too. I also attended the LaSalle Special Olympics for kids aged 7-15 (where I got to hand out prizes to the participants).

It was fun and fulfilling to "Quaker" for the kids. Looking back, I only wish I had it in me to do even more.

Chapter 14 – The Start of Basketball Season

During my time at Penn, the men's basketball team was the hottest ticket on campus. The year before I arrived, 1979, Penn's team, in the span of a week, defeated three top 20 teams in the NCAA tournament including perennial powers North Carolina, Syracuse and St. John's, to advance to the Final Four. This was virtually unheard of for an Ivy League team. At the send-off pep rally fans chanted, "Show no pity in Salt Lake City!"

Unfortunately for the Quakers, *they* were shown no pity in Salt Lake City as Magic Johnson's Michigan State team dashed their championship hopes with a 101-67 shellacking. In what would be the NCAA tournament's last ever consolation game, Penn ended its season with a loss to fellow semi-final loser DePaul in overtime 96-93. Nevertheless, the exuberance from Penn's deep run through the 1979 tournament led to high expectations and high demand for tickets in the years immediately following.

Students camped outside the ticket office in freezing cold weather beginning a full week before season tickets went on sale to snag the best seats. They would team up in groups, with each person taking shifts, so that someone from the group would always be present to keep their place in line while other members went to class or slept in a warm bed.

Fortunately, I never had to endure the pain of the season ticket line because, as a member of the band, I got free tickets. Because the band was so large, however, it was broken into three pep band groups and each group got tickets to only one-third of the games. Being the college basketball fan that I was, however, and wanting to see <u>all</u> the games, I would purchase the cheapest single tickets to the other games, wear my pep band shirt, bring my horn along and squeeze in with the band rather than sit alone in a different part of the Palestra. It made for some crowded seating, but no one ever questioned me or pushed me out.

One quick aside about the arena. The word "Palestra" is from the Greek for a public place for training or exercise in athletics. But to me, for the longest time I thought it meant "palace." When I learned the true definition, it really didn't change anything. The Palestra will always be a palace to me. And as the Quaker, I felt like the king of the castle.

As the Quaker, I got special treatment. I had a front row seat at all the Penn basketball games along with the rest of the cheerleaders. We sat courtside directly opposite the Penn team's bench. Also, all the security guards in the building knew me and would let me into the building whenever I showed up. This enabled me to go see other Big Five teams play when Penn wasn't. One of the more memorable games was when Villanova defeated 13th ranked Syracuse, led by future NBA player Dwayne "The Pearl" Washington, by two points before a packed house. Another time, I saw Villanova play Georgetown with future Basketball Hall-of-Famer Patrick Ewing as the Hoya's center. The Villanova fans taunted him incessantly including unveiling a rollout[23] during the game that read, "Can this you read, Ewing?"

---

[23] Rollouts were another Palestra tradition – usually reserved for games between Big Five teams and for games between Big Five teams and their archrivals. A rollout was a message written on a brown roll of paper that was 36 inches in height and could be as long as an entire row of seats on one side of the Palestra. Usually, two or three rolls were opened in sequence with each being passed down the stands after the message was delivered to the other side. Two of the more memorable rollouts for me were at:

1) The Penn-Villanova game following the arrest of Villanova's point guard, Stewart Granger, for allegedly being involved in the theft of furniture. The first rollout read: "Stewart Granger leads the Big Five in steals…" And the second read: "Sofas, chairs, tables, etc."; and

2) The Penn-Princeton game at Princeton during my sophomore year, which happened to be the only season Penn won the Ivy League and received the conference's automatic bid to the NCAA tournament. The rollout at Princeton was a sequel to the rollout that came out at Penn during the first meeting of the year between the two schools. The first rollout came at the end of a very heated game that Penn won 43-40 during which the Princeton fans chanted a very erudite "Penn Sucks" in response to Penn fans' chants of "Princeton's boooring!" The rollout came out in two parts. The first one read: "Ha, ha, ha…". The second: "[F@#k] you!" (but with the F-word spelled out in all its glory). The Penn administration had a fit! In advance of the game at Princeton a little over three weeks later, the Penn administrators issued a stern warning to Penn students threatening severe punishment if anyone repeated such behavior. The game at Princeton was just as hotly contested as the game at Penn and resulted in another 3-point Penn win. At the conclusion the game, out came a rollout that read, "Ha, ha, ha…" and we all held our breath as the second began to unfurl reading, "Well, you remember!"

But, of course, it was at the Penn games that I felt most beloved. The crowd, while still numbering in the thousands, was much smaller than the crowds had been at football games. Their proximity to the court made the whole experience more intimate. They really got into what I was doing and would cheer me on almost as much as they cheered on the team. And all the history and tradition in the building made it feel even more special.

One such tradition was handing (or tossing) out hundreds of red and blue streamers[24] to the fans as they took their seats. After Penn made its first basket of each game, the fans would throw the streamers in high arcs onto the court, stopping play until the cheerleaders and I cleaned them off the floor. Unfortunately, in 1985, other schools ruined this fun tradition by bringing other, more dangerous, things to throw and the NCAA banned the practice. Check out the next photo to see what the tradition looked like from the stands.

---

[24] Penn's colors are red and blue.

The streamers fly after the first Penn basket of the game in the Palestra.
Photo courtesy of the University of Pennsylvania Athletic Department

While the 1983-1984 season did not go particularly well for the basketball team,[25] there were some memorable Quaker moments.

Three out of the first four games were played at arenas in North Carolina, Texas, and California – too far away for the cheerleading squad to attend. Penn won its opener at Davidson but lost its next three including its home opener against Ohio.

Game five of the season, was played on a cold, mid-December Saturday afternoon against Loyola of Illinois, a team that featured the nation's second-leading scorer, Alfredrick Hughes. I was in costume and on the Palestra floor early that afternoon.

---

[25] They finished a disappointing 10-16 overall and 7-7 in the Ivy League.

There were very few people around – which is exactly what I wanted so that I could practice my juggling on the court. I was using white lacrosse balls so they would stand out against the colors in the arena.

While I was practicing, the Loyola players came out to start warming up for the game. Among those players, was a 6'10" backup center named Mike. Mike saw me juggling and called out, "Hey! I juggle, too. Give me those balls."

I hesitated and just looked at him. I didn't know if he was kidding or serious.

"C'mon!" he insisted waving his hands in front of his chest.

I relented and tossed the balls one at a time to him. Sure enough, he started juggling. Nothing fancy, but he kept all three balls in the air until his teammates called out, "Hey! Knock it off, Mike, and get serious over here!" Mike rolled the balls across the court back to me and took his place at the back of a line for layup drills. By this point, the crowd was starting to filter in and there were pockets of people in the stands. I had a thought.

I put the lacrosse balls back into my red and blue duffle bag and stood by the hoop at the end of the court that Loyola was using for its drills. When Mike got to the front of the line, I hopped out onto the court to cover him. Mike took a couple of dribbles forward, then stopped and shot the ball over me. He missed!

The people in the stands laughed and his teammates gave him all kinds of flak. They razzed him relentlessly, as he returned to the back of the line, for being "stopped" by a mascot. As he was moving up in line again, Mike called out to me to try it again.

I shook my head and said, "No way!"

But Mike insisted. "You have to give me a chance to redeem myself!"

With a deep sigh, I agreed to let him have another shot. Knowing full well that he was going to stuff it on me, I tried a different strategy. This time when Mike started dribbling, rather than just comically guarding him, I ran toward him and went for the steal. This took Mike by surprise, and I was able to get a finger on the ball. I didn't make the steal, but I did alter the course of the ball just enough to force Mike to go to his right to regain control of it before proceeding to the basket for a dunk.

Again, the crowd laughed at my near steal and his teammates gave him grief. He begged me again for one more chance. This time, however, I just shook my head and waved him off.

Once the game began, Loyola took an early lead. During the first timeout, I went to center court with my three white lacrosse balls and started throwing them in the air one at a time. I let them fall to the floor and bounce in different directions. I chased them all over the court. People laughed. I tried again. Same thing. The crowd grew restless. When the same thing happened for the third time, I earned what I had expected – boos from the crowd. At this point, per our pre-arranged plan, the male cheerleaders ran onto the floor, grabbed me, and rammed me (a la the goalpost routine) into one of the basketball posts. My apparent emasculation drew wild applause from the crowd.

During the second timeout, I returned to center court and began the same routine. This time, upon the first ball hitting the court, the crowd immediately booed. I held up my hands urging patience and returned to center court. I slowly began juggling successfully. The crowd cheered. As I increased the tempo of my juggling the cheering grew louder. Just as the buzzer sounded signifying the end of the timeout, I performed the Handless Catch and Toss Trick to perfection. After catching one of the balls on the back of my neck and tossing it back high into the air to continue my juggling, the crowd exploded in a frenzy of cheering.

The crowd's excitement and energy continued as the game resumed. The team seemed to thrive on the electric feeling and went on a 10-0 run to make it a close game. Alas, Penn was unable to sustain its effort and lost the game. But as the teams were leaving the court, one of the assistant coaches, Scott Beeten, said with a smile, "What did you do out there? You really got that crowd going!"

I explained what I had done, and Coach Beeten said, "C'mon with me. You're now a part of this team." He then led me into the team's locker room and assigned me a locker.

"You can give your costume to our equipment manager. He'll take care of getting it cleaned before games. And you can change and shower here," he said.

"Really?" I asked incredulously. "Thanks! I really appreciate it! By the way, Coach, I know the team is going to be playing in the Fleet Classic in Providence over winter break."

"Yep," he said.

"Well, I live in Connecticut. And if the team would put me up in the hotel, I'd be willing to drive there and perform at the games."

"Let me check on that," he said, and a few minutes later informed me that I was welcome to join them so long as I could get myself there.

Chapter 15 – The Fleet Classic

Four teams were competing at the midweek two-day Fleet Classic Tournament in Providence, Rhode Island: Penn, Providence, Rhode Island, and Temple. Penn was scheduled to play Providence in the opener on my birthday, December 28th. I left home late that morning, driving a 1970 brown Ford LTD to Providence.

When I got to the hotel, I found out I was rooming with Assistant Coach Scott Beeten who kept humming the chorus to Elton John's "I Guess That's Why They Call It the Blues" and breaking into full-throated song each time he reached the line, "Rolling like Thunder." I guess he really liked that phrase.

Anyway, a short time after checking in (and after about the 20th time through the song that Coach was humming and singing) we joined the team for the pre-game meal. It was 3:30 in the afternoon. Talk about an early bird special! But with game time at 7, we all needed time to eat and digest before taking to the court.

Coach Beeten and I walked into the hotel's dining room, which was virtually empty except for the team and the servers. He concluded his latest round of Elton's tune with "rolling like thunder," and we sat at one of several round tables. The other assistant coach, Tom Crowley, and some of the players were also at our table. There was a TON of food – hot rolls, salad, turkey, roast beef, potatoes, and a hot vegetable medley. There wasn't much conversation, but a lot of eating. By the time we had finished, it looked like a swarm of locusts had come through. Nothing left but empty plates and bones.

After the meal was complete, the team's head coach, Craig Littlepage, stood up and announced, "Everyone be back in the hotel lobby at 5. We'll board the bus then and head over to the arena."

At the announced time, the team, the coaches, and I clambered aboard the chartered bus that took us to the Providence Civic Center (today known as the Dunkin' Donuts Center). It was just a short ride from the hotel. I brought along my Penn Athletics gym bag filled with various props. The bus driver dropped us off just outside the civic center and we entered a side entrance that took us into a dimly lit, wide concrete hallway leading to our locker room. The team manager handed each of us our uniform as we came through the locker room door (mine being the only one with frills and knickers). We randomly chose lockers and changed from our street clothes into our game wear.

Coach Littlepage went over the advanced scouting report with the team. He spoke about who had recently been hot, and who not, on the Providence team. He talked about getting out on the guards and trying to deny passes inside to the big men. As he reviewed defensive assignments, he reminded players of their opponent's tendencies.

Upon finishing, Coach Littlepage said, "Hands in." Once the players all converged around him with hands touching high over their heads, coach yelled, "Let's go!" Breaking the huddle, the team made its way out to the hardwood to warm up. A good-sized crowd was already in the stands. In seconds, the rhythmic sound of bouncing basketballs interspersed from time to time with squeaks of sneakers gripping the floor on sudden stops and cuts by the players filled the arena. The Providence team appeared from the far corner, and it too began its warm-up drills.

In the meantime, I put my prop bag down at the end of the players' bench and took out my juggling balls. I juggled in the corner for a couple of minutes and then noticed that I had attracted a small audience of kids who had come to watch up close. Smiling, I put the balls back in the bag and high-fived my new fan club.

Seeing the Providence Friar out on the far side of the court, I turned back to the kids and held up my right index finger as I gave them a mischievous smile and quickly raised and lowered my eyebrows several times. I reached into my bag and pulled out a small towel. I tucked the towel inside my waistcoat and quickly strode across the court to shake hands with the Friar. Following our introductory pleasantries, I stood next to the Friar and together we watched the teams run through their drills.

While standing side-by-side, I grabbed the towel out of my coat with my left hand and brought it behind the Friar's back without him seeing it (his sight was limited by the large bald head he wore as part of his costume). I brought my arm up so that the towel was just above his head and, without turning my head away from watching the players on the court, I began moving the towel in small circles. Unbeknownst to the Friar, he was getting his head shined.

After a minute or so, I turned towards him, stood on my tiptoes, and "huffed" on the top of his head with one more rub of the towel to complete the job. The crowd was laughing, and I finally showed the towel to the Friar so he knew what was going on, too. I told him, "No charge," smiled, shook his hand, and retreated to the Penn bench.

As the game began, I looked around the arena and noticed that out of the thousands of fans in the stands, no more than a handful were Quaker fans. With that in mind, if I wanted to win over (or at least neutralize) the crowd, I needed to do things during the game that anyone could appreciate.

I returned to my bag and pulled out the parts to my kite. As I assembled it, my new fan club rushed back over to watch what I was doing.

I finished assembling my kite just in time for the first timeout. I dashed onto the court letting the kite out little by slow until it rose about 15 feet. I circled the court a couple of times with the kite in tow. The crowd roared. The kids in my fan club laughed as I returned to the sideline and winked at them.

Over the course of the game, I continued to entertain the the kids and the rest of the crowd by flying my kite, juggling, and playing with the Friar.

Penn ended up losing to Providence in a surprisingly close game 46-42. The result put Penn in the tournament's consolation game against the University of Rhode Island Rams – the school my high school buddy, Andy, attended. So, the next day, Andy and his girlfriend (now wife), Theresa, came to the game. They got there about a half hour before the game started so we had a chance to catch up for a few minutes. It was the first time they'd seen me in costume and in character. They couldn't stop smiling and ribbing me a little bit. It was great seeing them. At least I would know someone in the crowd.

Just before the start of the game, a member of the Penn radio station (WXPN) crew came over and asked if I would be willing to come up to the radio booth at halftime. I was caught completely off guard, but said, "Sure."

When halftime arrived, I climbed through the stands to the top level of the arena where the WXPN radio crew was stationed. There, sat Paul Jolovitz who was the play-by-play man.[26] While the station was broadcasting a commercial, Paul told me to take the seat next to him and to put on a set of headphones usually worn by his co-anchor, Neil Kaplan. I sat, took off my Quaker hat, put on the headphones, and put my Quaker hat back on.

What ensued was a nonsensical colloquy between a legitimate radio host and a wacked out mascot. At one point, Paul, growing a little exasperated with me, spoke directly to the audience, saying, "By the way, all of you in Philadelphia, nobody has ever accused this Quaker of being sane. That's one of the prerequisites for being the Quaker."

Throughout the interview, I remained hyped up in character and intermittently interrupted Paul and intentionally went off on

---

[26] Today, Paul is a well-known and well-regarded sports radio and television personality in the Philadelphia metro area. Possessing an encyclopedic knowledge about Philly sports, Paul (a/k/a Jolly) is a co-host of the WIP Philadelphia Eagles pre- and post-game shows, the WPHT and WIP Philadelphia Phillies pre- and post-game shows and is host of "Jolly Talk" on CBS 3 television.

zany tangents. At the end of the interview, Paul wrapped it up saying, "O.k., this has been Paul Jolovitz with Brian Becker on the halftime show. Thanks for being here, Brian."

"Thank <u>you</u>, Paul. Do I win a Gillette razor or something?" I asked.

"If you can find one," he retorted.

As I laughed and took off the headset, Paul continued, "Brian Becker the Quaker, our halftime guest. You can see why Brian is the Quaker. He's not normal on the court. He's not normal off the court. This has been Paul Jolovitz with Brian Becker, the Quaker. We're gonna send it back to Jerry Kranzel in the station now."

Following the commercial break, the broadcast resumed.

"Paul Jolovitz here at the Providence Civic Center, 40-25 the Quakers lead. Neil Kaplan back with me now. Brian Becker was asking if he got a Gillette razor. After that interview, I think <u>I</u> should get a Gillette razor or at least I should get the prize there. Neil, Brian Becker, a strange guy, but a very good Quaker."

Neil Kaplan responded, "Certainly is a great Quaker. And I think, as most of you listeners will know, this is the first time I have ever heard my trusted friend and colleague Paul Jolovitz upstaged during an interview. And I think, really, this is a momentous event."

It was the first time I was ever interviewed live on the air. It was quite the experience - apparently for them as well as for me!

Penn continued to play well in the second half and won the game 70-59. Following the game, I returned to Connecticut for the rest of winter break.

Chapter 16 – Back at the Palestra, a Memorable Weekend Visit, and Princeton Game One

The first game back in Philly after winter break was a Saturday night encounter with Big 5 foe St. Joseph's. Before the game, I approached the Hawk mascot (whom I had met when we visited the ill children at CHOP) to propose a three-part cartoonish plan that we could play out through timeouts and at halftime. He would "win" the first couple of times and I would "win" the last time. He readily agreed. We were set to perform.

When the first timeout was taken, I went to center court and began juggling. The Hawk swooped in, grabbed one of the balls I was juggling, and ran off. I gave chase but was unable to catch the speedy raptor as he disappeared beneath the stands and the St. Joe's fans cheered.

At the next timeout, I ran around the perimeter of the court flying my kite. The Hawk flew in and stole my kite. Again, he flew away and disappeared before I could catch him. As the St. Joe's fans roared, I threw my hat down in disgust and lightly tapped my forehead with my fist.

At halftime, with Penn trailing 38-31, I began the third act of our performance by walking out to mid-court and putting down a large paper shopping bag with "Bird Seed" written in large red letters on the two largest sides of the bag (facing the home and away sides of the stands). I then retreated to one corner of the court, stood alongside the Penn stands, and waited. I, along with the whole arena, watched as the curious Hawk stuck his nose into the bag and began eating.

While he was preoccupied with his snack, I stealthily crept up on him, lassoed him with a rope and dragged him off the court and under the stands to the cheers of the Penn fans. Moments later I emerged from under the stands with a giant cardboard drumstick while smiling and rubbing my belly. The Penn fans went wild! It was the biggest Penn cheer of the night as the basketball team provided little excitement and went on to lose by twenty points, 86-66.

Penn would lose another game, to crosstown foe LaSalle, before archrival Princeton came to town to play in the nightcap of a Palestra Saturday tripleheader. [27] The night before that game, my high school buddy, Andy, and his fraternity brother, John, came to Penn for a weekend visit. It would be an active weekend.

Saturday morning, I took Andy and John 10 blocks west of my off-campus house to a Philly jewel – Koch's Deli. Koch's was a family-owned sandwich shop where mom (Fran) and dad (Sid) Koch as well as sons Bobby and Lou all worked. Their motto was "More Meat for Less Bread."

---

[27] Penn-Princeton basketball games often decided the Ivy League Champion and, at the time, the recipient of the league's automatic bid to the NCAA Tournament. When Princeton rolled into the Palestra for this matchup, either Penn or Princeton had been the Ivy League Champion in 22 of the past 24 years. The rivalry was intense.

And let me tell you, they weren't kidding! Their mouth-watering sandwiches were ginormous. They had several different specials with multiple types of deli meat (a quarter pound of each type) on fresh bread or rolls. For example, the Lou Koch Special had roast beef, turkey, chopped liver, mustard or Russian dressing and onion on a double decker rye.

One's introduction to Koch's began on the sidewalk at the end of a line of people waiting to get in that stretched about halfway down the block from the front door. I told Andy and John not to worry. They wouldn't mind standing in line too much. The lengthy wait was made palatable, quite literally, by the piles of free deli meats and cheese on wax paper that got passed from the owners behind the counter down the line from customer to customer. This kept the hungry natives from getting restless.

The shop itself was a hole in the wall with just enough space on the customer side of the deli counter for the line of customers to snake from the front door to the back wall and around to the front of the deli case. At the turn, one of the Koch's would take your order and yell it to the other family members who were making the sandwiches. The whole time, there was constant chatter between the customers and the Kochs with plenty of jokes sprinkled into the mix. The Kochs made you feel like part of the family. The volume of free samples they doled out to the waiting customers was so great that I used to joke that by the time you got to the counter to place your order, all you would ask for was a napkin because you were so full. Andy and John were amazed by the place and by the size of the sandwiches.

With three sandwiches and a bag of chips in hand, we walked the ten blocks back to my rowhouse. We went into the dining room, poured some drinks, and began eating our brunch. Andy kept repeating how he couldn't believe the size of the sandwich before him. At about 220 pounds, Andy was a big boy. I thought he'd have no problem devouring the sandwich. I was amazed when he was only able to eat half the sandwich and declared he would save the rest for later.

As surprised as I was at Andy's inability to finish his sandwich, he was downright shocked when I finished mine. Knowing full well that I wouldn't have time to eat later before having to perform in the Palestra and knowing we had a house party happening after the game, I kept at it until I had inhaled the whole thing. Andy just stared at me in stunned disbelief wondering where it all went in my 165-pound frame.

Following brunch, it was off to the Palestra. A basketball tripleheader was on tap. Good thing Andy and John both loved college basketball. The afternoon games featured a MAAC matchup between Fordham and La Salle, followed by a tilt of A-10 rivals West Virginia and Temple. Given that Andy and John attended the University of Rhode Island (also an A-10 school), the A-10 game had some particular interest for them. Checking in with them between games, I found them really enjoying their Palestra experience.

I left them in the stands to go get dressed in the locker room before the final game of the day. Emerging from the locker room in costume, I happened upon a couple of cute Princeton cheerleaders on the sideline waiting for the rest of their squad to arrive. I took the opportunity to introduce myself and invited them to our post-game house party. They said they'd think about it and let me know.

The game itself began with the introduction of the starting lineups. But in the Palestra against Princeton, this was no routine introduction. While the Princeton players' names were being announced, you couldn't see a single fan's face on the entire Penn side. They were all hidden behind opened newspapers held straight up in front of them. The slow, methodical chant "BOOO-RIIIING, BOOO-RIIIING" accompanied the announcer's voice. When the announcer switched to introducing the Quakers, the fans quickly crumpled up their papers, threw them into the air and cheered each member of the Penn starting five.

The repetitive chant, "Princeton's Boring," would break out many times during the basketball game, too. "Why?" you might ask. Well, 1984 was the year BEFORE the NCAA introduced the shot clock[28] and Princeton's coach, Pete Carrill, was an adherent of the slow-down, often four-corner, offense designed to shorten the game by taking minutes off the clock with each position.

Princeton's game plan forced opposing teams to play defense for lengthy periods of time and bored the hell out of the fans. The Princeton players would lull their opponent's defense to sleep and then make a sharp backdoor pass for an easy layup. It was a brilliant tactic designed to keep what was often a less athletic team (Princeton) competitive with a more talented one. It worked exceptionally well in this game, too. The score at halftime was Princeton 21, Penn 14. Ugh!

At the intermission, I took to the court and performed the "Quaker School of Cooking" skit that I had developed during tryouts. And just like then, my audience laughed at the slapstick routine and roared when I reached into the pot and pulled out

---

[28] Initially, it was a 45-second shot clock, years later reduced to a 35-second shot clock, and today is now a 30-second one.

the rubber chicken as the last handmade sign revealed that what I had cooked was "Princeton's goose!" Unfortunately, for the basketball team, they couldn't say the same as they went on to lose the game 63-51.

At the end of every game, the cheerleaders faced the home side of the arena and led the crowd in the singing of The Red and Blue. Our singing was accompanied by choreographed moves involving arm motions and one foot moving forward and then back while other stayed stationery.   This proved to be the perfect opportunity for a Princeton fan sneak attack.

In the middle of the song, I felt my three-cornered hat leave my head. As I turned to look, I saw a male Princeton student in an orange sweater and blue jeans running across the court toward the Princeton side with my hat in one hand. I chased after him.

Just as the hat culprit was starting to climb back into the stands, I grabbed him by the back of his sweater, yanked him hard, and flung him directly into the arms of a Palestra security guard.

"I want him!" I yelled to the guard. "You got him," the guard replied as I ran up the stairs and chased the accomplices to whom the culprit had thrown my hat just as I grabbed him. Unfortunately, the accomplices had too much of a head start and got away.

I ran back to the basketball court as the guard took my captive to the security desk. I followed to formally lodge my complaint. As the guard behind the desk was getting the thief's information, a group of Princeton students burst through a door looking for their unfortunate friend. Two or three members of Palestra security fought to hold the intruders at bay.

"Where's the hat?" I demanded.

"Gone," one of them replied.

"Whaddaya mean "gone?"

"It's on a bus heading back to Princeton."

"Well, you better get it back, or your buddy here is gonna spend the night in a Philly jail." I threatened glaring at them. Philadelphia jails were known to be raucous and violent.

Panic ensued. The prisoner lost all the color in his face. His buddies were at a loss.

"It was just a fraternity prank," one member of the Princeton intruders offered.

"I can't go to a Philly jail! You guys have to do something," pleaded the poor preppie Princetonian who looked like he was going to crap in his pants.

"Nobody's going to jail," the security guard sitting at the table finally chimed in to quell the ruckus. "We'll just need to finish getting all of your information and then you can go," he said to the now profusely sweating thief.[29]

---

[29] As it turned out, the Princeton thugs did me a favor. You will recall that I had to stitch my hat back into shape after it got drenched in the pouring rain at Giants' Stadium. On the Monday following the Princeton game, I called the athletic department to report the theft and was instructed to contact Pierre's Costumes to get a new one, for which the Princeton athletic department ended up reimbursing Penn. So, in the end, I got a brand-new hat and Princeton paid the tab! Thanks guys.

At that point I left the Princetonians with the guards and returned hatless to the Palestra floor. There I found the two Princeton cheerleaders I had met before the game waiting for me with a guy they introduced as their "ride back to Princeton." They asked if it would be o.k. for him to come to the party, too. "Sure," I said, and after giving them the address, I went into the locker room, showered, and changed. Andy and John had already left. My housemates let them in when they arrived back at 4033 Locust Street.

I raced across campus arriving home as the party was starting to take off. I walked in the front door to find a mob of people. The music was loud, the beer was flowing, and Andy and John were trying to chat with some girls. When Andy saw me, he walked over, took a sip of his beer, and said, "Man, you were right. These girls are not friendly. They don't even want to talk to you never mind dance."[30]

"Uh huh," I said with a smile. "I told you! But there may be a couple of Princeton cheerleaders heading over."

"No way," was Andy's reply just as the front door opened and the two cheerleaders with their male driver friend entered the house. I introduced everyone and pointed our new guests to the keg.

---

[30] When Andy said I was right about the girls, he was referring to a conversation that he and I had over winter break. Andy had asked me why I still didn't have a girlfriend and I told him that it was tough at Penn. At the time seriously doubting me, he had retorted, "Yeah, right." After Andy's experience at this party, I felt vindicated.

We hung out in the living room drinking beer from the keg until the wee hours of the morning. After most of the party attendees had gone (including our guests from Princeton), I was sitting in a beat-up old chair across from the worn, green couch upon which John and Andy sat. Andy announced he had to "go tinkle," got up off the couch, and made a U-turn directly into the wall, completely missing the archway leading to the bathroom. We laughed until we cried!

After Andy returned from the bathroom, my housemate John (not to be confused with Andy's fraternity brother) came into the living room with a sheepish look on his face. "I just remembered," he said, "that we have an intra-mural basketball game this morning at 9." It was a little after 3 a.m. We looked at each other and decided we had better go to bed.

We were all hurting units when our 8:30 alarm went off. We threw on some sweats and groggily made our way through campus down to Hutchinson Gymnasium, located between Franklin Field and the Palestra. As we walked into the gym, our opponents were warming up on one of the several courts in the building. We grabbed some basketballs and started dribbling, passing, and shooting.

It wasn't pretty. On his first layup attempt, Andy ran towards the basket, put up the shot (he missed) and crashed into the padding on the wall behind the basket. Fortunately, he wasn't hurt. Even more miraculously, we ended up winning the game and my two Rhode Island guests (who obviously weren't even *on* our intramural team roster) were the top scorers that day!

We had a lot of fun that weekend and created some lasting memories. To this day, Andy and I shake our heads and laugh when we tell the story.

Chapter 17 – Another Chance to See My Parents and the Show Must Go On

Early February brought a road trip to southern New England to play Brown in Providence, Rhode Island on Friday night and Yale in New Haven, Connecticut on Saturday night. Since I was from Connecticut and knew my way (and since I was one of the few cheerleaders who was 21 – which was the minimum age necessary to drive the cheerleading van), I drove the van on the trip up. I don't remember much about it other than it was a long drive – especially with Friday afternoon traffic along I-95.

Somehow, we made it to Brown on time for the game, found Marvel gym, and did our usual energetic routines, which now included my running and going into a baseball slide when exiting from center court. Meanwhile the basketball team fell to the Bears 67-63. It was a disheartening defeat as it revealed how truly weak the team was in yet another rebuilding year. Immediately following the game, I drove the squad to our hotel in New Haven with most of the cheerleaders falling asleep along the way. I remember pulling into the parking lot a little before midnight, checking in, going up to the room I was sharing with another male cheerleader, pulling the room darkening curtains closed and collapsing into one the beds. I slept like a log.

The next thing I knew it was noon on Saturday. I couldn't believe it. After all, I am a morning person. It was the longest and latest I can ever remember sleeping. When I awoke, I was completely rejuvenated – and starving. After a huge brunch of eggs and toast, fruit, and pancakes, I joined the rest of the cheerleaders in a lounge area where we hung out and relaxed for most of the afternoon. We grabbed a light meal late in the afternoon before making our way to Payne Whitney Gym on the Yale campus.

Emerging into the gym, I saw my parents in the stands. They had driven down after work to see me perform again. I climbed into the stands and after exchanging hugs and kisses, I handed them each a streamer and explained what they should do with them after Penn scored its first basket.

During team introductions, I jumped all around the court as Penn's team was introduced, urging the few fans on the Penn side to shout their approval. As soon as the announcer began introducing the Yale team, I made myself at home by lying down on the court and dusting it with a pom-pom. I could hear my father's laughter and saw him pointing at me as I looked up with a yawn.

The game, itself, turned into another nondescript 4-point Penn loss. At its conclusion, I caught up with my parents again before heading off to change and drive back to Philadelphia. My dad told me the dusting bit before the game was "one of the funniest things I have ever seen." His comment made my night! I kissed them both goodbye and it was back to long-haul driving.

The winter cold and darkness, the long hours in the van, and the sporadic sleep took their toll on me. A day or two later I started feeling ill. By the following Wednesday, I had a fever of 101 degrees, a pounding headache, and a case of the sweats. It was a game night, however, and the show must go on! I was the only Quaker and felt I had to do my duty, particularly since it was a Big Five game against the Temple Owls. So, I dragged myself to the Palestra with a couple of extra props in tow.

During the first half of the game, I kept a relatively low profile. I just couldn't be my normal energetic self. I tried to stay away from people and kept going under the stands to drink fluids to replace the copious amounts I was losing through the perspiration that was drenching my costume.

Come halftime, I brought out the props I brought with me that night: a folding lounge chair; a sleeping bag; a borrowed teddy bear; a couple of signs that I had hastily made that afternoon; and a poster-sized thermometer I had drawn showing the mercury level at 101 degrees; and took to the court. I set up the chair with the sleeping bag on top of it, climbed into the sleeping bag with the teddy bear, and held up the first sign, which read: "The Quaker isn't feeling well." The crowd gave a loud "Awwwww!" I then held the giant "thermometer" up to my mouth showing the fans my 101-degree fever. This drew some laughter. Then I held up a sign asking for cards to be sent to me (see photo below taken from my yearbook, Poor Richard's Record). More laughter. Finally, I closed my eyes and pretended to nap.

Making the best of a bad situation. Still there even with a 101° fever.
Photo courtesy of Poor Richard's Record

My intention was to stay in this position throughout halftime, giving myself as much of a break as possible. Unfortunately, and much to my surprise, I felt the chair move! My eyes snapped open and when I looked up there was the Temple Owl dragging me toward the near basket. I felt some scraping and scrambled out of the sleeping bag and off the lounge chair. When I looked down, I saw large scrapes along the floor of the court. I yelled at the Owl calling him some choice names I won't repeat here and pointed out the damaged floor. Some maintenance workers tried to buff it out in the time remaining before the start of the second half without much success. I felt terrible both physically, from being ill, and emotionally because of the damage to the floor. Even though it wasn't my fault, I still felt responsible.

Penn lost a lopsided game 81-57. It actually worked to my advantage that there wasn't much to cheer for as I steadily felt worse as the night wore on. After the game in the locker room, I literally peeled my soaking wet costume from my fever-induced shivering body. After trudging home with my props, I fell into bed and slept dreamlessly until morning.

The sleep worked wonders and I was very lucky to be feeling much better by the next day. To my relief and delight, I felt back to normal by the time Cornell and Columbia rolled in for a pair of weekend games just two nights after the Temple game. If you were in the stands at the Temple game and again at the Cornell game, you would have noticed a big difference in my appearance, energy level and performance.

Before the Cornell game, I joined the basketball team on the court during warmups and sank three jumpers in a row from the side of the key while several players' shots bounced off the rim Seeing this, Coach Beeten yelled to me, "You're starting tonight!" I, and some of the team members, laughed. And then, I promptly missed my next two shots (more typical of my basketball prowess) and left the court for the sideline.

I was also happy to see that the maintenance crew's hard work between games had restored the Palestra's floor so that it was as good as new. The basketball team seemed to feel refreshed as well. They won both games.

There were only two memorable moments for me during those games. One moment was a silly bit I performed during a timeout in the Cornell game. I introduced a crazy character – Quintin Quaker – who was the Quaker's cousin and who was just visiting for the weekend. You can see Quintin, glasses and all, in the yearbook photo below. After being introduced,

Quintin vanished just as quickly as he arrived underneath the stands.

The Quaker's "cousin" makes an appearance.
Photo courtesy of Poor Richard's Record

The second moment was a mishap that occurred at the end of a timeout during the second half of the Columbia game. The cheerleaders dismounted from the human pyramid they had built and ran off the court. I followed with my now familiar run and baseball slide. Only this time, while I was in the midst of my slide, one of the female cheerleaders got off the bench and, without looking, stepped right into my path. There was nothing I could do but yell, "Look out!" But it was too late. My feet crashed into her ankles knocking her to the floor. I leapt up, apologized, and, along with a couple of other cheerleaders, helped her get up and move back to the bench. While shaken up, she was very fortunate to have suffered only a sore ankle.

Chapter 18 – Princeton Part Two and a Visit from the Budweiser Man

Basketball season continued. After a 24-point loss to crosstown rival Temple, and pair of Ivy League wins against Cornell and Columbia, it was on to Princeton for a rematch. Shortly after emerging from the locker room at Jadwin Gym, two Princeton Tiger mascots approached me. Rather than welcoming me to their homecourt like I had done with their cheerleaders at Penn, one Tiger was a real ass and threatened me.

"I'm going to steal your hat," he said (obviously ignorant of the Mascot Code that he shouldn't be speaking while in costume).

"No, you're not." I snapped back, "Because if you do, I am going to rip off your tail!"

That was the end of that. Nonetheless, I kept a wary eye out for others in the crowd who might try to steal my hat and I asked my fellow cheerleaders to be on watch as well. Fortunately, no attempt was made.

The game was a nail biter. Penn, having lost the first game, badly needed a win to stay in contention for the Ivy League title and an automatic bid to the NCAA tournament. The game started promisingly as Penn's defense was fierce and they fought their way to a 22-17 halftime lead.

With the Penn crowd feeling buoyant, I carried out the longstanding tradition of Quakers going to center court with a series of alternating pairs of handwritten signs. The first sign of each pair would always read, "I like Princeton…". This invariably drew boos from the Penn crowd. The second sign of each pair would read, "but then I like" – and then, something distasteful would be added such as "rubbing myself with maple syrup in the middle of an ant farm." This was met with applause and/or guffaws."

I took to center court and produced the following pairings:

I like Princeton…
but then I like running barefoot through broken glass!

I like Princeton…
but then I like drinking from a fire hydrant!

I like Princeton…
but then I like raw hamburger on mint chocolate chip ice cream!

And finally,

I like Princeton…
but then I like Brooke Shields's eyebrows.[31]

This latest combo hit the mark! The Penn crowd loved it! Penn fans were hyped up as the teams returned to the court.

---

[31] Shields was a film celebrity who was attending Princeton University at the time and who had bushy eyebrows so thick they made you think she had Neanderthal relatives.

The second half, however, proved to be painful. After Penn extended its 5-point lead to 7 with just over 12 minutes to go in regulation, the offense went cold, free throws were missed, and regulation play ended in a 36-36 tie. Penn lost in overtime 45-41. The opportunity for an Ivy title was essentially gone.

After the game, the very pretty Princeton cheerleaders who had come to our off-campus party following the first Princeton game at Penn, and their equally beautiful roommates, invited me to stay for dinner. I desperately wanted to accept their invitation with visions of staying overnight with them (after all, it *was* Valentine's Day). But flashing through my mind, I couldn't help but think that it might be a trap to not only steal my costume, but also to hold me hostage (I could imagine some big guys jumping out of bushes to grab me). Also, it occurred to me that I didn't have a credit card or sufficient cash to get myself back to Philly. I regretfully turned them down, but often wondered what would have happened had I stayed.

The season proceeded with Penn playing just under .500 basketball the rest of the way. After defeating Harvard, the team suffered a rare home Ivy League loss to Dartmouth.

Then Villanova came to the Palestra and defeated the overmatched Quakers 65-51. It was a far cry from Penn's 84-80 victory over the Wildcats the year before, in which Penn guard Anthony Arnolie hit 10 straight free throws to seal the win. Nevertheless, in hindsight, it was amazing to share the court with 10 Villanova players who would go on to defeat heavily favored Georgetown the following year to win the National Championship. I particularly remember tapping a loose ball to future NBA star Ed Pinckney during the pre-game warmups.[32]

Following an 0-2 road trip to Columbia and Cornell, Penn returned home to play Yale and Brown on the final weekend of the season. About a half hour before the start of the Yale game, I was on the court organizing my props when the Yale Bulldog sauntered over to say hello. While we were exchanging pleasantries, a "professional" mascot, The Budweiser Man, dressed in what looked like a red batman type outfit came over to us.

With his chest puffed out, Budweiser Man declared, "I'm here tonight boys! And I'm going to be doing some things out on the court during the game, so stay out of my way!" He turned on his heels and strutted away.

"What an a-hole!" I said under my breath to the Bulldog. Thinking quickly, I added, "Wanna get him?"

"What do you have in mind?" the Bulldog asked. I shared my plan with him, and he readily agreed.

During the first timeout in the basketball game and without so much as giving us a look, the Budweiser man charged out to center court and, facing the Penn crowd, began his bold, manly routine. In the meantime, the Bulldog and I met over at one end of the court. Using a rope, I put a "leash" over the Bulldog's head and took him for a walk. The Bulldog, on all fours, strode next to me as we ambled toward midcourt. I kept my gaze on the visitor side of the arena as we approached the Budweiser Man from behind.

---

[32] The 6'9" Pinckney would go on to play in the NBA from 1985-1997.

When we got to the Budweiser Man, we stopped and with me still looking up at the Yale crowd pretending not to know what the Bulldog was doing. He lifted his left hind leg and proceeded to "piss" on the Budweiser Man. The crowd erupted in laughter. I turned slowly toward the Budweiser Man who still had no idea what was going on and was completely confused by the crowd's reaction to his performance. I raised my hands in feigned shock at the Bulldog's action. The crowd laughed harder. The Budweiser Man finally saw what had caused the crowd's sudden hysterical outburst as I pulled the Bulldog away from him. I scolded the Bulldog and wagged a finger at him. Then I returned to the Budweiser Man's side and in a large motion pulled a hankie from my pocket. I knelt next to him and began wiping his leg with the hankie while waving my other hand apologetically. This garnered more guffaws from the audience.

As I wiped the stunned Budweiser Man down and pretended to apologize for the Bulldog's behavior, I said through a smile, "Don't f@#k with us! This is MY home court! The next time you want to do something, ASK first!" I rose, high-fived the Bulldog, and returned to the sidelines with the crowd cheering wildly.

The Budweiser Man slinked off the court and went under the stands where he remained for most of the game. Late in the contest when a timeout was called, with lesson learned, the Budweiser Man meekly approached me and asked if he could go out on the court. "Sure," I replied. "Thanks," he said. And that was that.

The following night was the season finale against Brown. It started, as usual, with the starting lineup player introductions.

Unlike all the other games, however, the starting lineup on this night included all the seniors on the team. Below is a photo of little-used guard Brad Wynn being introduced as a starter in his last game at the Palestra. I joined the team in congratulating him as he took the court.

Senior Night introductions.
Photo courtesy of Poor Richard's Record

It being my last home game as well, I prepared a special, personal timeout moment for my swan song. When Coach called a timeout with only a few seconds left in the game, the cheerleading captain turned to me and said, "Brian, the court is yours!"

With that, I ran to center court for the last time and held up signs that read:

"And now it is time to go"

"Where all good Quakers go…"

"Penn Law School!"

The Palestra erupted in applause. And then I slid out from behind the last sign a little extra sign that read:

"Please?"[33]

The crowd responded with some laughs and some "Awwwwws" as I shrugged, ran, and went into my baseball slide off the court for the last time.

---

[33] At the time, I was still awaiting the law school's response to my application.

Chapter 19 – Going Out in Style

With the end of basketball season, there were only two months to go before my Penn experience would be over. It proved to be a bit of a blur. Spring break came and went. As usual, I went home. I never could afford to make the trip south to hang out on a beach like so many others did, but I never felt deprived.

Then there was Spring Fling and my last appearance as the Quaker on campus at the grand opening celebration. I shared the stage with University President Sheldon Hackney and looked out on the throngs of happy, drunk students. It reminded me of a scene from a Spring Fling performance of The Mask and Wig Club[34] which I had tape recorded and memorized because I listened to it so much. In that scene, one of my

---

[34] Per the club's own website: The Mask and Wig Club, founded in 1889 by Clayton Fotterall McMichael, is the oldest all-male collegiate musical comedy troupe in the United States. Founded as an alternative to the existing theatrical and dramatic outlets at the University of Pennsylvania, Mask and Wig has presented comedy, music, and dancing to the University of Pennsylvania, Philadelphia, and audiences across the country. The Club's performers, or "The Cast" stage two all-original shows each year in collaboration with the Club's own Stage Crew, Band, and Business Staff. The Club's primary purpose has always been and continues to be, "Justice to the stage; credit to the University."

favorite performers, Lew Schneider[35] played the Right Reverend Dr. Oral Hygiene. One of his lines went something like, "As I look out upon this fine student body, I see a number of fine student bodies. And I'd like to get to know each of them personally!" Lew and the whole troupe were hilarious. Lots of fun! And now I saw what Lew had seen from the Sping Fling stage.

In addition, while up on the stage with President Hackney, I saw one of the DP's photographers, Dan Schmutter, shooting this photo:

On With It

WITH ALL THE SPIRIT of a modern-day Greek demigod, President Sheldon Hackney officially kicked off Spring Fling yesterday in the Lower Quadrangle. But Quaker Brian Becker is less than impressed, and seems to wish that the president would get off of the podium and into the dunking booth.

As soon as Hackney finished his opening comments, I jumped off the stage to catch Dan and asked him to

____

[35] Lew went on to Second City and a career as a stand-up comic, an actor, a writer, and a producer for a number of television shows, including, most famously, Everybody Loves Raymond.

accompany me to the law school dean's office. I hoped another creative appeal might earn me acceptance into the school. Dan accommodated me and shot this photo that appeared in the DP the following Monday:

Alas, my ploy proved fruitless. I wound up getting waitlisted at Penn and ended up going to Boston University instead. This turned out to be quite fortuitous, but more on that later.

Following finals, was senior week. It was a week filled with fun activities such as: the Walnut Walk where you tried to have a drink at every bar on Walnut Street in Philadelphia from Front Street all the way back to campus (which I attempted to do with a number of friends – we got seriously drunk, but we all made it back to campus alive); the dance down the Delaware (an event in which there was drinking, dinner and dancing on a ferry that slowly motored down the Delaware River); a pitch and putt outing (my first time playing any kind of golf other than miniature – and I didn't finish last in my group); and a special treat, an NCAA lacrosse playoff game at Franklin Field in which sixth-seeded Army (unfortunately) defeated third-seeded Penn 8-7 after an Army player speared Penn's leading scorer in the first quarter knocking the star player out of the game.

The week was a perfect bookend to orientation week freshman year, which likewise had been packed with a bunch of fun activities. As anyone who has studied psychology can tell you about the effects of primacy and recency, people tend to best remember the first events and the last events in any given sequence. By creating fun, festive environments at the beginning and end of our Penn careers, my friends and I theorized that the arrangement was designed to create a lasting, positive imprint on us. This, in turn, would make it easier to solicit donations from us as we ventured forth in our lives. To this day, I think it was a brilliant tactic – and it worked!

Interspersed with all the fun activities, I slowly, reluctantly began packing up my belongings. while listening to music and wishing I didn't have to leave. Even though I knew the fun time couldn't go on forever, I wasn't ready for it to end. Yet I tried to lighten my mood by dressing for the occasion. Check it out…

Wearing "formal attire" to pack during senior week.
Photo from author's personal photo collection

Despite trying to wish it away, graduation day did arrive. Our graduation ceremony was held inside the Philadelphia Civic Center, which was located right on the edge of Penn's campus just down the street from Franklin Field. With thousands of graduates and their families in attendance, I decided to wear my three-cornered Quaker hat to help my parents find me. I brought along my mortar board, too, so I'd be able to join my classmates in moving the tassel from one side to the other when Sheldon Hackney pronounced us graduates.

Here are a couple of photos of my housemates and me outside the Philadelphia Civic Center on graduation day. You'll notice the Quaker hat in the first photo. It served its purpose, as my parents later told me they were able to pick me out in the crowd.

Housemates heading to graduation.
Photos from author's personal photo collection

Over the years, Penn frequently featured amazing graduation speakers, including U.S. presidents, vice presidents, U.S. Supreme Court justices, other high-ranking government officials, entertainment celebrities, world-renowned activists, and the like. We were excited at the prospect of hearing from a notable luminary at our graduation. The person(s) in charge of booking our graduation speaker, however, made a major mistake and had to scramble at the last minute to find someone. That someone turned out to be the mayor of Philadelphia, W. Wilson Goode – a mere year before his infamous order authorizing the bombing of a Philly neighborhood. The choice of Mayor Goode was met with outrage by most of the student body and apathy by the rest. In a constellation of stellar graduation speakers, the mayor ranked right up there with a 40-watt lightbulb.

In large part due to the uninspiring graduation speaker, the graduation ceremony itself was boring. The most notable part, aside from us graduating, was an empty chair draped in a doctoral gown with a cap on the seat representing Andre Sakharov, a Soviet nuclear physicist, dissident, Nobel laureate, and activist for disarmament, peace and human rights who was in internal exile in the city of Gorky and upon whom Penn was conferring an honorary doctorate. A shot of Sakharov's chair appeared on the CBS Evening News that night. Too bad he couldn't have been the graduation speaker.

Because of the size of the university, President Hackney had each school stand when called, pronounced us graduates, instructed us to move our tassels from right to left, and invited us to take our seats. Since I, like many of my fellow graduates, had absolutely no interest in hearing Goode's commencement address, and since we had to go to the registrar's office after the ceremony to pick up our diplomas, and since I still had to finish loading my belongings into the rented U-Haul, and since it was a four-plus hour drive back to Connecticut following graduation, I decided not to stay for the remainder of the ceremony. Instead, I bolted from the Civic Center and ran to the registrar's office.

As the clerk in the registrar's office handed me a cardboard cylinder with my diploma ensconced inside, she congratulated me and told me that I was the first one to receive a diploma that day. Ever since, I've told people that "I may not have graduated with distinction, but I don't care who graduated *magna cum laude* or *summa cum laude*, I graduated *first* in my class."[36]

-----

[36]This quote was memorialized on page 177 of my yearbook, Poor Richard's Record, in a piece entitled, "Quaker's Corner, An Interview with Brian Becker." The interview was conducted post-graduation over the phone by a friend of mine, Bruce. Among the things he asked about was whether I agreed with a quest started during our senior year to change the words of a favorite Penn song, "The Red and Blue" by eliminating references to Yale and Harvard. I said while it would be nice to get Harvard and Yale out of our song, it didn't really matter to me. As part of my answer, I took the opportunity to address another crazy student pursuit. This latter movement was an attempt to change the name of the university. The advocates were students who were upset by people's confusion between Penn and Penn State. Those students wanted to change the name of the school to Franklin University to honor our founder, Ben Franklin. I said, "We can't do that because when people ask, 'where do you go to school,' we'd have to say, "F.U.!"

The confusion between Penn and Penn State, however, is real. While the difference is clear to those who need to recognize it, such as graduate schools and employers, it can pose problems to those less sophisticated. The funniest example of this confusion was an episode during my sophomore year.

After leaving the registrar's office, I returned to 4033 Locust Street where I met up with my parents who were still glowing from the commencement - hugs, kisses, and smiles all around. We finished loading the U-Haul with my belongings and I drove the truck with my dad riding shotgun. It felt weird to be leaving Philadelphia no longer a Penn student.

Dad and I were chatting as we cruised along in the left lane of the New Jersey Turnpike when suddenly dad said, "You better move over. There's a cop with his lights on coming up behind you." I moved over. So did the cop.

I looked at my speed and was not going over the speed limit. My dad saw that, too, and just as dad said, "He can't be coming for us," the cop flashed his headlights. Bewildered, I pulled over onto the shoulder of the highway. The police car pulled behind us.

———————————

It was a Saturday morning, and I was standing outside the Quad waiting to cross Spruce Street on my way to the band room when a car pulled up. A young woman rolled down the passenger-side window and asked me where such-and-such hall is (I can't remember the actual name). When I told the young woman and her mother (who was driving) that I hadn't heard of such-and-such hall, they produced a map and told me that the young woman had an interview there in 30 minutes.

The map they produced showed the building they were looking for on a university campus. The name of the university at the bottom of the campus map, however, was Penn State. Upon seeing this, I informed them that they were going to be very late for the interview as they were about 200 miles east of where they needed to be! I wished them good luck and left them with their jaws hanging.

I rolled down the driver's side window as the New Jersey State Trooper walked up. He asked for my license and a copy of the paperwork for the truck. I asked what was wrong and he replied that I had been illegally driving the truck in the left lane. Dad and I looked at each other as neither of us had seen a sign stating that trucks were prohibited from the left lane. My dad spoke up. "Officer, he just graduated from college today and we didn't see any signs," he said hoping the officer might acknowledge the special occasion and let us go with a warning.

No such luck. The trooper was unmoved. I turned over my license and the paperwork. The trooper walked back to his squad car. After what seemed like an eternity, he returned to my window with a ticket featuring a hefty fine. Talk about a damper on the celebratory mood. Welcome to the real world!

Chapter 20 – You Can Take the Man Out of the Quaker Costume, but…

Despite leaving Penn, the Quaker experience continued to play a role in my life. It keeps popping up from time to time in different ways. I'd like to share just a few standout examples.

As I mentioned earlier, it was a good thing I didn't get into Penn Law School. Turns out it was during my first year at BU law school, that I met my future wife, Laura, in the law library.[37] We were engaged two months after our first date. A few months later, after having finished playing an intramural game of flag football, I caught up with Laura in a neighborhood laundromat. I was wearing a long sleeve t-shirt with a navy-blue background and white "Pennsylvania 84" lettering. As we were folding the fresh-out-of-the-dryer laundry, I looked up and noticed a guy across the laundromat staring at me. Suddenly, he exclaimed, "You're the Quaker!"

The look of surprise on Laura's face was priceless. I laughed and calmly replied, "I *was* the Quaker, but I'm not anymore." I introduced Laura as my fiancée, at which time the guy blurted

---

[37] There was a reason I wasn't meant to attend Penn Law School and a great one at that! ☺

out, "Do you know who you're marrying?!" Laura and I looked at each other and laughed as we still had only been together a few months at that time – but we didn't tell that to our star-struck observer. We later joked with one another that the answer (had she given one) would have been, "Not really."

Laura and I were married on May 25, 1986. When we arrived in our apartment following the wedding, we exchanged wedding presents. I gave Laura a beautiful Japanese jewelry box. She loved it. See for yourself.

My gorgeous bride opening her wedding gift.
Photo from author's personal photo collection

Then she gave me my present. I kid you not, it was a bed sheet. See for yourself.

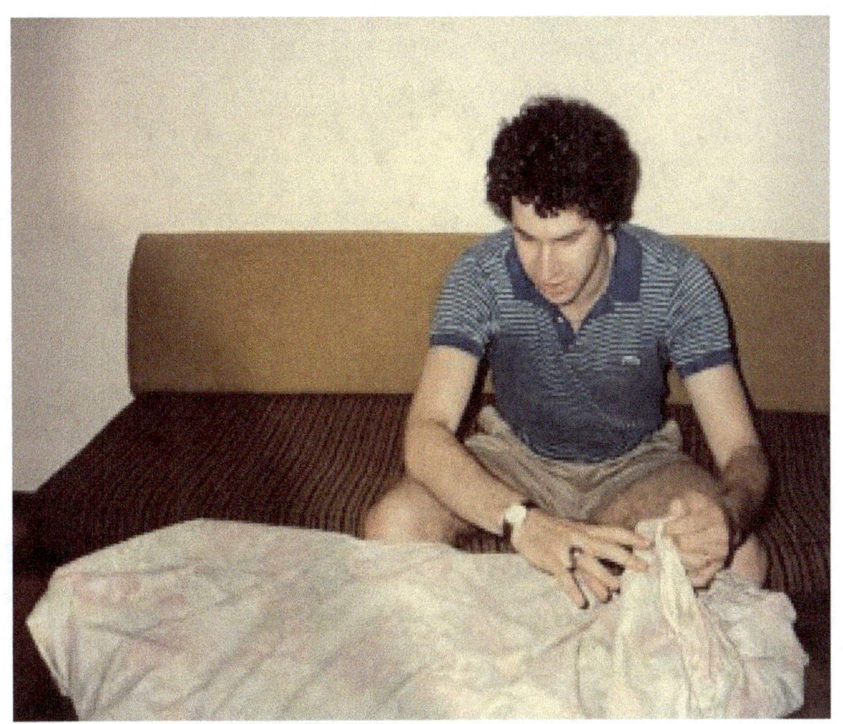

A bed sheet for a wedding present?
Photo from author's personal photo collection

But wait, there was something in the bed sheet…

Much to my amazement, it turned out to be MY QUAKER COSTUME!!! It was the actual costume I wore. You could even see the area on the knickers that I had worn out sliding all around the basketball courts.

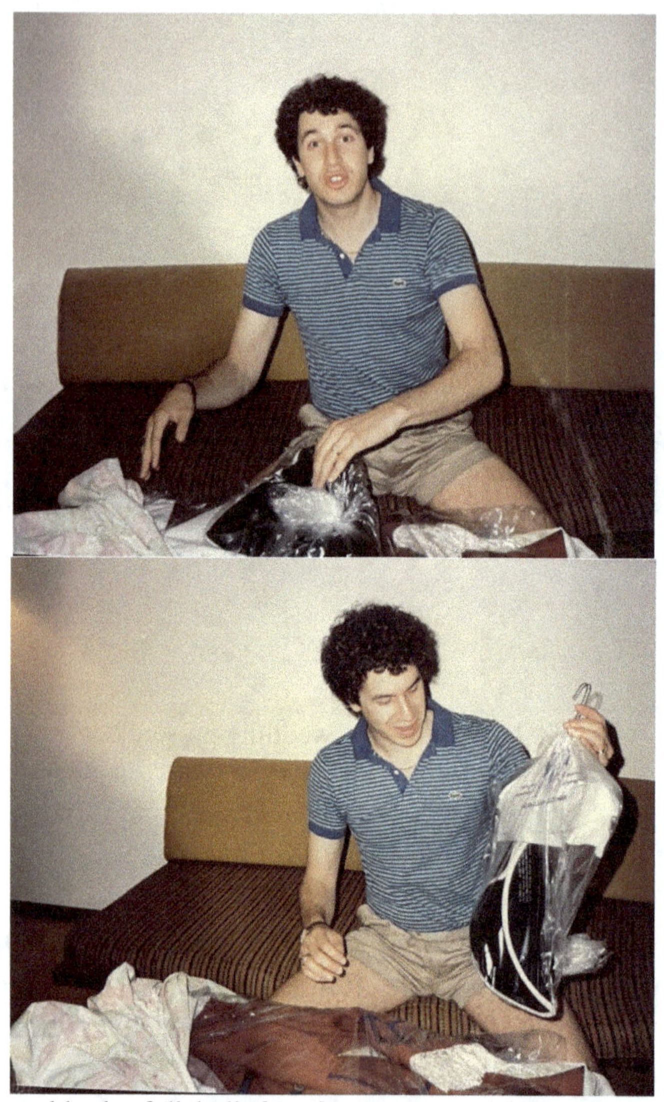

Stunned look of disbelief as the contents within are revealed.
Photos from author's personal photo collection

An INCREDIBLE gift! I was dumbfounded. When I asked my lovely bride how she had obtained MY costume, she told me that the idea had occurred to her at the Penn/Harvard football game I took her to see at Harvard Stadium in the fall after we met.

While we were sitting in the stands, I pointed out the Quaker and told her, "That was me, except that's a new costume he's wearing." She filed that thought away. A few days later, Laura called the Penn athletic department, explained that she was going to be marrying me, that she learned the school had purchased a new mascot costume and asked what they had done with the old mascot costume. After learning that it was just sitting somewhere in storage, she asked if she could acquire it as a wedding present in exchange for a donation to the university. The deal was struck, and the costume was hers. And now, she gave it to me!

I was 24 years old when Laura and I got married. The Quaker costume would hang in a closet for the next 16 years. I brought it out only on a few rare occasions when I told the story to a guest for the first time. I also showed the costume to my sons, Casey and Cary, when I shared tales about my being the Quaker.[38]

When I turned 40, Laura surprised me yet again! This time, after sneaking the costume out of the house and having it carefully dry-cleaned, she presented it to me in a handsome custom-made box frame suitable for hanging in a museum. Now, it proudly hangs above the Daily Pennsylvanian homecoming article on a wall in our home.[39] See for yourself.

---

[38] For those of you who might have seen me perform the goalpost routine and were kind enough to worry about its potential long-term effects on my reproductive health, my sons are proof that it still works!

[39] My hope is that perhaps someday, when I am long gone and no one in my family has any desire to display these two framed pieces, the University will accept them and find a corner in the Palestra in which to hang them.

A unique display at home.
Photo from author's personal photo collection

It's quite the conversation starter when people come to our home for the first time! After learning that I was the Quaker, people often ask me questions about the experience. When they do, I share some of the same stories that I have shared with you in this book.

There was one other particularly noteworthy surprise stemming from my being the Quaker. In 2010, I was elected to the Connecticut House of Representatives. Each legislator is assigned an office in the legislative office building adjacent to the State Capitol. I hung the framed DP homecoming article in my office. It served as a nice icebreaker with folks who came to visit me as well as with my new colleagues in the legislature.

One of those new colleagues, Chris Donovan, the then Speaker of the House, apparently took special notice of my wall decoration. I was unaware of this until Chris Perone, a veteran House member, showed up in my office and told me that the Speaker had assigned him to be my mentor. As Chris sat in my office, an inscrutable look appeared on his face as he stared at the framed article on the wall.

After a moment, I broke the silence. "Do you think it was a mistake for me to put up the article?"

"No, no." Chris replied with a chuckle. "It's perfectly fine."

"Then what's with the look on your face?" I asked.

"Oh, nothing." Chris responded. "The Speaker has a sense of humor. I now understand why he matched us up."

"What do you mean?"

After another chuckle and a pregnant pause, Chris revealed, "Well, you see, I was the Syracuse Orange!"

"You're kidding!" I blurted out smiling at the coincidence. "That's amazing."

And I think that single word just about sums up the whole Quaker experience. Amazing!

9 798218 232498